NATIONAL UNIVERSITY
LIBRARY

Vista Library

# Shakespeare and the Experience of Love

# Shakespeare and the Experience of Love

ARTHUR KIRSCH

CAMBRIDGE UNIVERSITY PRESS

*Cambridge*
*London   New York   New Rochelle*
*Melbourne   Sydney*

Published by the Press Syndicate of the University of Cambridge
The Pitt Building, Trumpington Street, Cambridge CB2 1RP
32 East 57th Street, New York, NY 10022, USA
296 Beaconsfield Parade, Middle Park, Melbourne 3206, Australia

© Cambridge University Press 1981

First published 1981

Printed in the United States of America

Library of Congress Cataloging in Publication Data
Kirsch, Arthur C.
Shakespeare and the experience of love.
Includes bibliographical references and index.
1.  Shakespeare, William, 1564–1616 – Criticism and
interpretation.   2.   Love in literature.   I.   Title.
PR3069.L6K5          822.3'3          81-635
ISBN 0 521 23825 0                    AACR2

*To
Alice, Matthew,
and
Beverly*

# Contents

| | | |
|---|---|---|
| Preface | *page* | ix |
| 1 | Introduction | 1 |
| 2 | *Othello* | 10 |
| 3 | *Much Ado About Nothing* | 40 |
| 4 | *Measure for Measure* | 71 |
| 5 | *All's Well That Ends Well* | 108 |
| 6 | *Cymbeline* | 144 |
| 7 | Conclusion | 174 |
| Notes | | 181 |
| Index | | 193 |

# Preface

Central to my understanding of the treatment of love in Shakespeare has been the assumption that the plays represent elemental truths of our emotional and spiritual life, that these truths help account for Shakespeare's enduring vitality, and that they deserve direct critical attention. My primary focus is on the relevance to the plays of Christian and Freudian approaches to these truths, not as systems intended to diagnose moral or psychological pathology, but as analogous means of understanding the profound experiences of love Shakespeare depicts and the sources of their tragic, comic, or tragicomic energy and design.

It is fashionable now to be skeptical about our capacity to establish any truth within or about a literary text, and it is evident enough that theological and psychoanalytic interpretations of Shakespeare can be dispiritingly reductive, doctrinaire, and remote from literary experience. But these abuses are not inescapable. Theological and psychoanalytic ideas need not be applied in pointless attempts to diagnose Shakespeare's own psychical or religious makeup, nor need they be employed as remorseless engines of judgment. They can instead be used to enhance our understanding of the experience that transpires within the plays and that the plays elicit from us, and I think that if literary study is not to become increasingly solipsistic and arid, we should draw more, not fewer, relationships between literature and experience. Christian and Freudian ideas are far more spacious and humane than the uses to which literary critics have normally put them, and joined together they can illuminate Shakespeare's meaning in terms that are as pertinent to

ix

Renaissance thought and feeling as to ours. The real problem is one of critical tact, and I hope that my own interpretations of the plays will seem temperate as well as true.

The chapter on *Othello* first appeared as "The Polarization of Erotic Love in 'Othello'" in *The Modern Language Review*, 73 (1978), pp. 721–40. It is slightly revised in this book. The chapter on *Measure for Measure* is a revision of "The Integrity of *Measure for Measure*," *Shakespeare Survey 28* (Cambridge, 1975), pp. 89–105. The chapter on *All's Well That Ends Well* contains material from *Jacobean Dramatic Perspectives* (Charlottesville, 1972), but it is essentially a new argument.

My work was aided by grants from the American Council of Learned Societies and the University of Virginia. I have been helped by many friends and colleagues, and by my students, particularly those in my Shakespeare seminars. Lester Beaurline, David Bevington, Alastair Fowler, E. D. Hirsch, and Norman Rabkin read parts of the book and gave me the benefit of their criticism and encouragement; and Jeffrey Cox and Joyce Van Dyke stimulated and helped me crystallize some of my ideas in the early stages of writing. I owe a special debt to Donna Landry, who read a preliminary draft of the entire manuscript and made numerous valuable suggestions. I also wish to thank Patricia Emlet and Jessie Shelar for their help in preparing the manuscript for publication.

# 1

# Introduction

Dr. Johnson wrote in the *Preface to Shakespeare* that

Shakespeare is above all writers, at least above all modern writers, the poet of nature; the poet that holds up to his readers a faithful mirrour of manners and of life. His characters are not modified by the customs of particular places, unpractised by the rest of the world; by the peculiarities of studies or professions, which can operate but upon small numbers; or by the accidents of transient fashions or temporary opinions: they are the genuine progeny of common humanity, such as the world will always supply, and observation will always find. His persons act and speak by the influence of those general passions and principles by which all minds are agitated, and the whole system of life is continued in motion. In the writings of other poets a character is too often an individual; in those of Shakespeare it is commonly a species.[1]

Johnson expands upon these thoughts to explain Shakespeare's continued appeal to audiences and readers:

As his personages act upon principles arising from genuine passion, very little modified by particular forms, their pleasures and vexations are communicable to all times and to all places; they are natural, and therefore durable; the adventitious peculiarities of personal habits, are only superficial dies, bright and pleasing for a little while, yet soon fading to a dim tinct, without any remains of former lustre; but the discriminations of true passion are the colours of nature; they pervade the whole mass, and can only perish with the body that exhibits them. The accidental compositions of heterogeneous modes are dissolved by the chance which combined them; but the uniform simplicity of primitive qualities neither admits increase, nor suffers decay. The sand heaped by one flood is scattered by another, but the rock always continues in its place. The stream of time, which is continually washing the dissoluble fabricks of other poets, passes without injury by the adamant of Shakespeare.[2]

These familiar passages are worth taking at face value, and seriously. I think what Johnson says about Shakespeare's characters is true. They do "act and speak by the influence of those general passions and principles by which all minds are agitated and the whole system of life is continued in motion," and their power and endurance in dramatic literature is indeed attributable to the "colours of nature" that pervade them and to the "primitive qualities" that they embody.

Johnson's thoughts can easily be domesticated in neoclassical criticism, but they also echo creative preoccupations both of the Renaissance period and ours. By "primitive qualities," it is clear that Johnson means those that are primal, elemental; and he associates such qualities equally with psychological and spiritual experience – with the passions that compose our emotional life as well as the principles that govern our moral one. He also suggests that such primitive qualities exist as a part of a whole system of life that is continued in motion because of them. In the Middle Ages and the Renaissance such a primal conception of character and experience rested on Christian theology and was characteristically expressed in ideas like that of the psychomachia, which was understood as a dynamic system of moral forces. In our own times, a psychological conception of character and experience is more habitual, and it finds expression in ideas such as Freud's notion of the unconscious, which is understood as a dynamic economy of psychic forces. As Johnson assumes in the preface, the two systems or economies of human experience are frequently analogous, and I think that both are at work in Shakespeare's plays.

In *Speak Memory*, Vladimir Nabokov refers (contemptuously) to "the fundamentally medieval world of Freud."[3] Its intent aside, his analogy is suggestive. The demonstration of the wisdom or usefulness of combining Freudian and Christian ideas in interpreting Shakespeare must depend ultimately upon my analyses of particular plays. For the moment, in this introduction, I wish simply to suggest that a simultaneously psychological and religious conception of human experience was immediately available to Shakespeare in the form he would have most valued, in the traditions of the medieval morality and mystery dramas that were the inheritance of his own stage. These traditions have frequently been discussed in Shakespeare scholarship, but often with the fruitless intention of proving specific influences and reducing Shakespeare to them. The real importance of medieval drama to Shakespeare was larger and deeper, for the early theater was the creative nucleus of his own most fundamental conceptions of dramatic character and action.[4]

In 1639 a man named Ralph Willis described a performance of a morality play called *The Cradle of Security*, which he had witnessed as a boy almost seventy years earlier, in about 1570. It is a performance such as Shakespeare and his audience might have seen in their own childhoods as well as in later years, because moralities continued to be played well into the seventeenth century.

In the city of *Gloucester* the manner is (as I think it is in other like corporations) that when players of enterludes come to towne, they first attend the Mayor to enforme him what noble-mans servants they are, and so to get licence for their publike playing; and if the Mayor like the actors, or would shew respect to their lord and master, he appoints them to play their first playe before himselfe and the Aldermen and common Counsell of the city; and that is called the Mayor's play, where every one that will comes in without money, the Mayor giving the players a reward as hee thinks fit to shew respect unto them. At such a play, my father tooke me with him and made mee stand betweene his leggs, as he sate upon one of the benches where wee saw and heard very well. The play was called (the Cradle of Security) wherin was personated a king or some great prince with his courtiers of severall kinds, amongst which three ladies were in speciall grace with him; and they keeping him in delights and pleasures, drew him from his graver counsellors, hearing of sermons, and listning to good counsell, and admonitions, that in the end they got him to lye downe in a cradle upon the stage, where these three ladies joyning in a sweet song rocked him asleepe, that he snorted againe, and in the meane time closely conveyed under the cloaths where withall he was covered, a vizard like a swines snout upon his face, with three wire chains fastned thereunto, the other three end whereof being holden severally by these ladies, who fall to singing againe, and then discovered his face, that the spectators might see how they had transformed him, going on with their singing.

Whilst all this was acting, there came forth of another doore at the farthest end of the stage two old men, the one in blew with a serjeant-at-armes his mace on his shoulder, the other in red with a drawn sword in his hand and leaning with the other hand upon the others shoulder; and so they two went along in a soft pace round about the skirt of the stage, till at last they came to the cradle, when all the court was in greatest jollity; and then the foremost old man with his mace stroke a fearful blow upon the cradle, whereat all the courtiers, with the three ladies and the vizard, all vanished; and the desolate prince starting up bare-faced, and finding himselfe thus sent for to judgement, made a lamentable complaint of his miserable case, and so was carried away by wicked spirits.

This Prince did personate in the Morall, the Wicked of the World; the three Ladies, Pride, Covetousnesse, and Luxury, the two old men, the End of the World and the Last Judgement. This sight tooke such impression in me that, when I came towards mans estate, it was as fresh in my memory as if I had seen it newly acted.[5]

As F. P. Wilson has remarked, no effort of historical imagination can entirely recapture this man's experience and enable us to see the moralities as he and his contemporaries did, but his account is nonetheless unusually eloquent and suggestive. It reveals, to begin with, the familiar point, that in morality drama the characters "personate" abstractions, that they are conceived as personifications of moral qualities – pride, covetousness, lechery, and so forth. It is also evident that for Willis these personifications had enormous concrete vitality. He remembers them, as Wilson remarks, "first and foremost" as a king and three ladies and two old men.[6] At the same time, however, there is no indication that the palpable life of the characters was discontinuous in his mind from the abstractions they signified. The "moral" to Willis is both the moral of the story, as we would now say, and the story itself. And that story, we should remember, is ultimately a depiction in concrete images of an action *within* the soul of the play's protagonist, the "king or some great prince." The three ladies are projections of parts of him,

and their action on the stage represents his own internal move-
ments. The "sight," therefore, which makes so deep an impression on Willis that it remains fresh and moving to him after
seventy years, is a dynamic image of the interior of a human
soul, of the interaction of precisely the qualities within a human
being that Johnson called "primitive" and we ourselves might
call "primal."

The sense of a mental landscape that is as psychological as it is
moral may have to be inferred in *The Cradle of Security* because
the play is not extant, but it is plain enough in a great morality
such as *The Castle of Perseverance*. The unique staging of *The
Castle of Perseverance* is itself suggestive. The image presented in
the drawing that has come down to us – of Mankind's castle, with
his bed under it, surrounded by the scaffolds of God, the World,
the Flesh, Belial, and Covetousness – literalizes the scaffolding
of a human life and reflects the same allegorical impulse, if not
essentially the same mental topography, that is to be found in
Freud's diagrams depicting the composition of the psyche. The
action of the play evokes such a topography with great scope as
well as richness of detail. We witness the panorama of Mankind's spiritual progress from birth to death and judgment, and
in the course of that progress we are introduced to virtually all
the "general passions and principles" that can be thought to
animate a human life. The cast of characters alone presents us
with a conspectus of elemental human experience: Belial, and
with him Pride, Wrath, and Envy; Flesh, and with him Glut-
tony, Lechery, and Sloth; Covetousness, Backbiter; Shrift, Peni-
tence; Meekness, Patience, Charity, Temperance, Chastity,
Business, and Generosity; Death; the Soul (after Mankind's
death); Mercy, Truth, Righteousness, and Peace; the Father sit-
ting in his throne.

Mankind himself, Humanum Genus, and with him the Good
Angel and the Bad Angel, has an active role in the play, but
though he sometimes interacts directly with the other characters, he often does not, and the level of his awareness of other
characters varies considerably. I think these distinctions of in-

teraction and awareness are in some sense equivalent to modern
psychological distinctions between conscious and unconscious
activity, but in any case Humanum Genus is ultimately inseparable from almost everything that happens in the play. Most of
the action is not only about him, it constitutes him. He exists as a
separate character, with all the definition and vitality an actor
could give him; but he is also, if not finally, made up of the
primitive impulses and energies of the forces that are represented in the characters surrounding him. The play as a whole
thus composes as well as decomposes his "personality." The
other characters, the set, and the action are visualizations of the
processes of his experience, and these processes are primal.
They comprise the essential life of all men. Humanum Genus
himself is one man and all men.

Such allegorizations of human experience accustomed medieval theatrical audiences to a way of understanding the primitive
components and processes of human behavior, which Freud, in
a sense, had to recover through psychoanalytic excavation. This
understanding persisted to a significant degree in the Renaissance, and it is therefore not unreasonable to assume that in a
play like Othello, for example, Shakespeare could have intended
and expected his audience to understand the three central
characters (if not the others also) as composing a single moral
and psychic entity, Desdemona and Iago being conceived as
expressions of discrete elemental forces within Othello. Nor is it
alien to what we can infer about the expectations of spectators
trained by the moralities to assume that Shakespeare could have
wished them at the same time to respond to all three characters
as powerfully particularized individuals. Moreover, because
Shakespeare was free to explore the dramatic ideas of the
morality independently of their specific homiletic origins, the
relation itself between the two senses of character in his plays is
fertile and suggestive.

The other profound source of nourishment for Shakespeare
and his audience in the medieval dramatic tradition was the
mystery plays. Though they were not performed after the mid-

dle of the sixteenth century, primarily because of Protestant objections to the theatrical representaticn of Papist idols, Shakespeare would have perceived their essential form in the manifold effects they had in the evolution of Tudor drama, and they are as truly the ancestors of his own plays as the moralities are.[7] The mysteries develop a resonance of dramatic character and experience not unlike that of the moralities, though less through characterization than through action. Characters like Mak and the three shepherds in *The Second Shepherds' Play* are represented as realistic entities, specifically as imitations of English shepherds, in a way that morality characters do not seem to be, but the whole configuration of the action, including the so-called double plot, invests them with a metaphysical amplitude and purpose. The shepherds' laments at the start of the play, for example, are personally defined, but they also express a more generalized spiritual condition – the state of isolation and joylessness in a world unredeemed by Christ; and the subsequent intrigue with Mak, in which the shepherds at first wish to punish him and then, in the deeper spirit of their gift to his child, to forgive him, represents at once the birth of charity within them and the birth of Christ Himself, which makes that charity possible. The transformation of the English shepherds into the shepherds outside Bethlehem is thus, like the Nativity, immanent in the play from the start, and the whole of the play represents a continuous process of psychic as well as spiritual change.

I shall try to show later in more detail that there are many unusually rich analogies between a play like *The Second Shepherds' Play* and the primary psychic processes that are reflected in what Freud called "dream-work," including the conception of time and the immanence of the dream-wish in the construction of the whole dream, but at this point I would suggest only that both join together the transcendental and the ordinary, and with comparable mechanisms of expression. The conflation of a literal sheep and the Lamb of God in Mak's child is a perfect instance of dream condensation, and the way in which the whole plot of Mak and the shepherds not only parallels the Nativity but enacts its meaning is an example of dream displacement. And in the play, as in a dream, both mechanisms provide a means, as well as an expression, of the experience of transformation.

Such conceptions of dramatic experience as these remained alive on the English stage long after the mystery plays and their direct representations of scriptural history had disappeared. They helped form the theatrical sensibility of Shakespeare and his audience, and they clearly provided some of the resources for Shakespeare's own extraordinary dramatizations of human experience. They are especially helpful in explaining the motives and construction of his comedies and romances. In *Much Ado About Nothing*, for example, as in the medieval mystery drama, the multiple plots have a symbiotic relationship. The spiritual reverberations of the story of Claudio and Hero are displaced onto, as well as realized through, the largely psychological energies of the plot involving Benedick and Beatrice, and both plots draw nourishment from the comedy of Dogberry, whose childlike receptivity to experience suggests the ancestry of the shepherds in *The Second Shepherds' Play*. All three plots together represent the play's informing experience, which is the transformation wrought in men and women when they are in love. Similarly, in *Cymbeline* the whole plot involving Cloten is a displacement that both makes possible and expresses the psychic and spiritual process of Posthumus's return to his love for Imogen, and as in *The Second Shepherds' Play* that individual movement is dilated into an image of a regenerated human community.

The filaments that connect medieval and Renaissance drama, of course, are extremely diverse and complicated. They comprise a vast subject in themselves, and one that I do not pretend to explore in this study. I have wished only, in these few pages, to suggest that the moralities and mysteries provided a reservoir of primal dramatic thinking for Shakespeare and his audience that makes it historically plausible to draw upon both Renaissance theology and Freudian psychology in interpreting the experience and design of his plays. The ultimate justification for such an approach, however, is the validity of the interpretations themselves.

In the chapters that follow, I will examine five plays in detail: *Othello, Much Ado About Nothing, Measure for Measure, All's Well That Ends Well,* and *Cymbeline.* They form an extremely coherent group at the same time that they span a significant portion of Shakespeare's career and reflect his work in various genres. All five are manifestly concerned with erotic experience in a way that naturally encourages both psychological and religious interpretation. *Much Ado About Nothing, Othello,* and *Cymbeline* are almost evolutionary developments of an identical erotic motif: jealousy is the spring of the action in all of them; the heroes have many and deep affiliations, as do the heroines and tempters; and the plays have profoundly similar emotional and spiritual cadences. *Measure for Measure* and *All's Well,* which have long been associated as problem comedies, are developed in a distinctly different key, but the heroes and heroines still have much in common with those of the other three plays: the tempters, though muted and more mundane, are still present, and though jealousy is not at the center of the action, its psychic and spiritual concomitants are. Like *Much Ado, Othello,* and *Cymbeline,* the problem plays are fundamentally concerned with the dialectic between narcissism and idolatry on one hand and love and faith on the other. In all five plays the resolution of that dialectic depends upon a sacramental conception of marriage, and romantic love itself, as I shall try to show, is ultimately represented as a modulation of charity. There are, of course, other Shakespearean plays, notably the other romantic comedies and final romances, that deal similarly with erotic experience, but these five are representative, and they have rich and illuminating analogies.

# 2

# *Othello*

*Othello* is composed of an extraordinary mixture of antithetical states of feeling and being. The extremes are literally as well as emblematically represented in Desdemona and Iago, but they are most deeply incarnated in Othello himself, who moves from one to the other, from the transcendence and love celebrated in the first half of the play to the nearly utter disintegration and hatred dramatized in the second half. The contrast is so drastic that most critics find it insupportable. *Othello* is not the only Shakespearian tragedy to dramatize such oppositions (*Lear* especially does), but *Othello* poses a peculiar difficulty for critics because its preoccupations are so unremittingly sexual. At the core of *Othello*'s conception of execution is an uncomfortably intense focus upon the sexual relationship between a man and a woman in marriage, a relationship that was as inherently paradoxical and mysterious to Elizabethans as it is to us. It is a mystery celebrated in many of the Petrarchan conceits that *Othello* literally enacts,[1] but its essential paradox is most explicitly and profoundly described in the words of St. Paul that are cited in the marriage liturgy:

So men are bound to love their own wives as their own bodies. He that loveth his own wife, loveth himself. For never did any man hate his own flesh, but nourisheth and cherisheth it, even as the Lord doth the congregation: for we are members of his body, of his flesh and of his bones. For this cause shall a man leave father and mother, and shall be joined unto his wife, and they two shall be one flesh. This mystery is great, but I speak of Christ and of the congregation.[2]

Referring to the Bible, Freud describes the same mystery in approximately analogous terms: "A man shall leave father and mother – according to the Biblical precept – and shall cleave to his wife; then are tenderness and sensuality united."[3] He explains that "to ensure a fully normal attitude in love," the union of both "currents" of feeling is necessary, and that this union is ultimately derived from a child's early symbiotic relationship with his mother in which his love for her and his love for himself are identical.

I think we should attend to both St. Paul and Freud in interpreting *Othello*. Existing theological and psychoanalytic criticism of the play admittedly does not offer an especially encouraging precedent: apart from being grossly reductive, most of it is driven by the impulse to convict Othello of moral or psychic failure. Because Othello's energies and conflicts are not diseases to be cured or redeemed, such an impulse inevitably deforms the play. But the quest for pathology is not an inescapable function either of Christian or psychoanalytic thinking, and both systems of thought can be used to illuminate the experience of the play, rather than vice versa.

In *Troilus and Cressida* Hector warns Troilus that it is "mad idolatry / To make the service greater than the god" (II. 2. 56), and that play in fact depicts a world in which madness and idolatry do characterize all sexual and social relationships. It is essential to recognize at the outset that the world of *Othello* is different, that Desdemona is not Helen or Cressida, that she is true, and that there is no service greater than she deserves. One would suppose these to be self-evident propositions, but there are notable critics who dispute them. A. P. Rossiter, for example, actually equates Desdemona with Helen, indicts Othello for ascribing "false excellences" to her, and dismisses her as a "pathetic, girlish, nearly-blank sheet."[4] W. H. Auden responds to her more fully, but thinks even worse of her. "Everybody must pity Desdemona," he writes:

but I cannot bring myself to like her. Her determination to marry Othello – it was she who virtually did the proposing – seems the romantic crush of a silly schoolgirl rather than a mature affection; it is Othello's adventures, so unlike the civilian life she knows, which captivate her rather than Othello as a person. . . . her deception of her own father makes an unpleasant impression. . . . she seems more aware than is agreeable of the honor she has done Othello by becoming his wife. . . . Before Cassio speaks to her, she has already discussed him with her husband and learned that he is to be reinstated as soon as is opportune. A sensible wife would have told Cassio this and left matters alone. In continuing to badger Othello, she betrays a desire to prove to herself and to Cassio that she can make her husband do as she pleases. Her lie about the handkerchief is, in itself, a trivial fib but, had she really regarded her husband as her equal, she might have admitted the loss. . . . Though her relation with Cassio is perfectly innocent, one cannot but share Iago's doubts as to the durability of the marriage. It is worth noting that, in the willow-song scene with Emilia, she speaks with admiration of Ludovico and then turns to the topic of adultery. . . . Given a few more years of Othello and of Emilia's influence and she might well, one feels, have taken a lover.[5]

Auden's response is deeply perverse, but I have cited it at such length because in sophisticated or disguised form his assumptions and prejudices subsume more criticism of the play than might at first be apparent. Though I suppose few readers of *Othello* (and still fewer of its spectators) would even conceive of faulting Desdemona for not being "sensible," there are many who do feel that she is too good to be true, too innocent to be a wife or too wifely to be innocent, and this attitude is quite as damaging to the play as Auden's outright hostility. Either way, the play eventually starts turning inside out. It is therefore important to any interpretation to pay detailed attention to the terms in which Shakespeare presents Desdemona and not to take her for granted.

The first substantial impression we receive of her is in Othello's description of their courtship. He tells how he often visited her father's house, how he recounted the story of his life at Brabantio's request, and how he drew from Desdemona a "prayer of earnest heart" to tell that story to her:

> I did consent,
> And often did beguile her of her tears,
> When I did speak of some distressful stroke

That my youth suffer'd. My story being done.
She gave me for my pains a world of sighs;
She swore, in faith, 'twas strange, 'twas passing strange;
'Twas pitiful, 'twas wondrous pitiful.
She wish'd she had not heard it; yet she wish'd
That heaven had made her such a man. She thank'd me;
And bade me, if I had a friend that lov'd her,
I should but teach him how to tell my story,
And that would woo her. Upon this hint I spake;
She lov'd me for the dangers I had pass'd;
And I lov'd her that she did pity them.

(I. 3. 155)[6]

The tenor of Othello's whole speech, as well as the Duke's reaction to it ("I think this tale would win my daughter too" [I. 3. 171]), should alone suggest that Desdemona is hardly an overaggressive schoolgirl, that their wooing was delicately mutual, and that in responding to the story of Othello's life she was responding to the man it revealed; but an even more important index of her characterization is the description of the precise nature of her response. After centuries of sentimentalist thinking, we may be disposed to regard tears and the capacity for pity as cheap commodities, but Shakespeare did not. Pity is always exalted in the plays (the Italian word "pietà" may perhaps better suggest its Shakespearean connotations), and it is regularly the most compelling virtue of his heroines. It is incarnated in Cordelia when she returns to Britain, as she says, to "go about" her father's "business," weeping and praying:

All blest secrets,
All you unpublish'd virtues of the earth,
Spring with my tears; be aidant and remediate,
In the good man's distress.

(IV. 4. 15)

It is inscribed in Miranda's characterization at the start of *The Tempest* when she laments to her father, "I have suffered / With those that I saw suffer," and he tells her to calm her "piteous heart" (I. 2. 5–6, 14). Desdemona's feeling for Othello is of this kind. It is a sign not that she is silly or guileful, but that she has a capacity to sympathize deeply with human suffering, that she has a piteous heart.

Desdemona enters immediately after Othello's speech and her father asks her, "Do you perceive in all this noble company / Where most you owe obedience?" The moment is charged both for those on stage and for us, and the impact and importance of her answer, the first words she speaks in the play, cannot be exaggerated:

> My noble father,
> I do perceive here a divided duty:
> To you I am bound for life and education;
> My life and education both do learn me
> How to respect you; you are the lord of duty –
> I am hitherto your daughter; but here's my husband,
> And so much duty as my mother show'd
> To you, preferring you before her father,
> So much I challenge that I may profess
> Due to the Moor, my lord.

> (I. 3. 179)

These luminous lines, which are strongly reminiscent of those that Cordelia uses when she defies Lear,[7] evoke the very cadence of the scriptural injunction to marry: "For this cause shall a man leave father and mother, and shall be joined unto his wife, and they two shall be one flesh"; and Desdemona's description of the transfer of her feelings from her father to her husband, with its invocation of her own mother as her example, touches in almost archetypal terms upon the psychological process by which a girl becomes a woman and a wife. These associations are unmistakable, and Desdemona's strikingly unusual choice of a husband only heightens their power. Othello's age, possibly the same as her father's, literalizes the psychological reverberations, and his blackness, as we shall see, intensifies the theological ones. It is nonsense to imagine that Shakespeare created such a speech for a character who was to be an unpleasant homiletic example, a "caution," as Thomas Rymer put it, "to all Maidens of Quality how, without their Parents consent, they run away with Blackamoors."[8]

It is even greater nonsense to imagine that such a speech would introduce a girl incapable of "mature affection." As Desdemona immediately shows, she loves Othello as a wife should, body and soul. She insists on going with him to Cyprus in a speech that is even more remarkable for its spiritual and emotional poise than her first:

> That I did love the Moor to live with him,
> My downright violence and storm of fortunes
> May trumpet to the world. My heart's subdu'd
> Even to the very quality of my lord:
> I saw Othello's visage in his mind;
> And to his honours and his valiant parts
> Did I my soul and fortunes consecrate.
> So that, dear lords, if I be left behind,
> A moth of peace, and he go to the war,
> The rites for why I love him are bereft me,
> And I a heavy interim shall support
> By his dear absence. Let me go with him.
>
> (I. 3. 248)

There are few instances in Shakespearean drama of so explicit, so natural, and so harmonious an integration of flesh and spirit. Sensuality and affection are inseparable in Desdemona's consciousness. She loves Othello to live with him; she acknowledges but is unashamed of the violence of her behavior; she wants to consummate the marriage; she is subdued to Othello's very quality ("utmost pleasure" in the quarto). At the same time, she consecrates her soul to his honor and valiancy, and says that she "saw Othello's visage in his mind." That charged and crucial statement cannot be fully appreciated apart from Othello's characterization, and I shall return to it, but for the moment we can at least observe that it testifies to a kind of spiritual "eyesight" that Shakespeare consistently celebrated in his other plays. The presence of this vision in Desdemona authenticates her desire for Othello and is an expression of the fullness as well as the transcendence of her love. It is also a measure of her own surpassing worth as an object of love.

Desdemona's subsequent appearances in the play only confirm and heighten these initial impressions of her love and of its value. In the scene of her arrival in Cyprus, Cassio refers to her as "the divine Desdemona" (II. 1. 73) and calls upon the men of Cyprus to kneel in adoration of her. At the same time he speaks of her in explicitly sexual terms:

> Great Jove, Othello guard,
> And swell his sail with thine own powerful breath,
> That he may bless this bay with his tall ship,
> Make love's quick pants in Desdemona's arms,
> Give renew'd fire to our extincted spirits,
> And bring all Cyprus comfort!
>
> (II. 1. 77)

That Cassio, as we later see, is incapable of unifying such idealized and sensual feelings in his own erotic life does not diminish the force of his perception of their union in Desdemona, and her sexual integrity is particularly radiant in this scene. In response to Othello's fear during their reunion that "not another comfort like to this / Succeeds in unknown fate," she says:

> The heavens forbid
> But that our loves and comforts should increase
> Even as our days do grow!
>
> (II. 1. 192)

The pellucid beauty of these lines, as of so many others that Desdemona speaks, is a function of the harmony of instinctual and spiritual life that Shakespeare represents in her, and it is characteristic that she should see the passage of time not as a threat to marriage but as a promise of its growth and fulfilment.

The promise, of course, is never fulfilled, and in the remainder of the play, as Iago pours his pestilence into Othello's ear, Desdemona becomes increasingly incapable not only of comforting her husband but even of understanding him. Many critics besides Auden interpret this failure as evidence of her own inadequacy. Whatever merit such a judgment might have in our lives outside the theatre, in the world of the play it is the opposite of the truth, as Iago himself explicitly informs us:

So will I turn her virtue into pitch;
And out of her own goodness make the net
That shall enmesh them all.

(II. 3. 349)

Iago is a liar, but not in his soliloquies, and Shakespeare gives us no reason to doubt him here. Quite the contrary, for our constant apprehension of how Desdemona's virtues are perverted is central to our response not only to her but to the entire action. She is human, she has a literal identity, and it is possible to discover considerable stubbornness in her disastrous advocacy of Cassio, but to stage or read those scenes in which she pleads for Cassio as the exercises of a wilful woman or a domineering wife is to misconstrue her motives and to become as subject to Iago's inversions as Othello does. Her fundamental concern is not for Cassio, for whom she does nevertheless feel love, but for her husband, for Othello. She intuits, what we after all know, that Othello's alienation from Cassio is unnatural and injurious to them both. She sees Cassio as Othello's devoted friend, "That came a-wooing with you, and so many a time, / When I have spoke of you dispraisingly, / Hath ta'en your part" (III. 3. 72), and she begs Othello to forgive him in the terms and for the reasons that truly prompt her:

'Tis as I should entreat you wear your gloves,
Or feed on nourishing dishes, or keep you warm,
Or sue to you to do a peculiar profit
To your own person.

(III. 3. 78)

She is thinking, as ultimately she always does, of Othello, not of herself, and the conclusion of her plea is: "Be as your fancies teach you; / Whate'er you be, I am obedient" (III. 3. 88). And she is. She obeys Othello literally until death parts her from him.

She also continues, in the words of the liturgy, to love and honor him, and much of the horror and pity we experience at the end of the play comes from our perception of the ways in which her absolute fidelity to marriage helps destroy it. She misplaces the handkerchief in the first place because she cannot comprehend Othello's allusion to the pain in his forehead, and she uses it to bind his brow and to comfort him. It is he, in his distemper, who brushes it aside and "loses" it. The same innocence is the source of her persistence in pleading for Cassio while Othello asks her about the handkerchief, thus more deeply associating the two in his mind, and of her general incapacity to recognize and therefore cope with his jealousy. That innocence, as her wondering discussion of adultery with Emilia makes clear, is born of her own absolute marital chastity.[9] She may unconsciously apprehend more of what Emilia believes than she realizes, as her corruption of the willow song seems to suggest,[10] and she is human enough, in mentioning Lodovico as a "proper man," to have intimations of a marriage that might have been better than her own, for she senses what is to come. She is also, certainly, momentarily terrified of dying (for which some critics, for some unfathomable reason, fault her), but her last words are for Othello, and her earlier bewilderment and fear only heighten our sense of the depth of her love, the monstrousness of its destruction, and the overwhelming pity of its loss. The worldly Emilia testifies, at the cost of her life, to the truth we ourselves most deeply feel: "Moor, she was chaste; she lov'd thee, cruel Moor" (V. 2. 252).

The peculiar integrity and power of Desdemona's characterization, as I have been suggesting throughout this discussion, are in part a function of the literalness of her exemplification of the religious and psychological commitments of marriage. As a result she is the most domestic of Shakespeare's heroines at the same time that she is one of the most elemental and numinous, and in the latter half of the play her symbolic overtones become particularly insistent. Othello compares her to a chrysolite, which was one of the twelve precious stones in the walls of the heavenly city (Rev. xxi, 20) and was traditionally associated with faith, constancy, and innocence, "all things in Christ";[11] and in his final speech, when he realizes how much he has lost, he speaks of her as a pearl, and his own image suggests the pearl of great price (Matt. xiii, 45–6).[12] Toward the end, a profusion of references associates her with heaven and salvation, and the more Othello sees and treats her as a devil, the more saintly she seems and becomes. In the worst of her suffering, as she kneels to Iago for help, she says:

> Unkindness may do much;
> And his unkindness may defeat my life,
> But never taint my love.
>
> (IV. 2. 160);

and she remains sacrifically true to that love as she dies:

> EMILIA: O, who hath done this deed?
> DESDEMONA: Nobody. I myself. Farewell.
> Commend me to my kind lord. O, farewell!
>
> (V. 2. 126)

It is this kind of love, with its manifold religious and psychological reverberations, to which Othello first responds and with which his own love resonates in the first two acts of the play. In these acts he and Desdemona are so well tuned that they seem together to be an elemental expression of that single state of being toward which marriage aspires, and his characterization cannot be understood apart from hers. His blackness and his age especially, his two most salient features, have enormous symbolic as well as literal significance in their marriage. In any performance his color and its contrast with Desdemona's are visually most powerful, and images of darkness and light permeate the language of the play. As G. K Hunter has shown, there were two opposing conceptions of the black man in Elizabethan England.[13] The first was the primitive and ancient sense of black as the color of inferiority and wickedness, which was incorporated in early Christian eschatology and became deeply ingrained in Christian thinking. In medieval and Renaissance drama and art, devils as well as evil men (the torturers of Christ, for example) were regularly depicted as black. It is this sense of blackness that Shakespeare's audience would most likely have brought to the theatre and that, with a particularly acrid emphasis upon sexual bestiality and unnaturalness, is strongly associated with Othello in the first few scenes of the play. The play opens with a cascade of obscene references to Othello's color and race ("thicklips," "a Barbary horse," "the gross clasps of a lascivious Moor," "a gross revolt" [I. 1. 67, 113, 127, 135]), and Iago tells Brabantio explicitly that

> Even now, now, very now, an old black ram
> Is tupping your white ewe. Arise, arise;
> Awake the snorting citizens with the bell,
> Or else the devil will make a grandsire of you.
>
> (I. 1. 89)

The "spiteful old pantaloon"[14] Brabantio himself picks up the litany. He expresses disbelief that Desdemona could have "run from her guardage to the sooty bosom / Of such a thing as thou – to fear, not to delight," and repeatedly states that only pagan witchcraft, the "practices of cunning hell," can explain how "perfection so could err / Against all rules of nature" (I. 2. 70; I. 3. 102, 100).

The other Elizabethan conception of blackness, more peculiar to Christian theology and less familiar now, was the notion that all men are black in their sinfulness, but become white in the knowledge of the Lord, a belief that was especially adumbrated in evangelically tinted voyage literature, which treated inferior and black-faced foreigners as creatures whose innocence made them close to God and naturally prone to accept Christianity. The root metaphor of this attitude was drawn from the Song of Songs and the belief found expression as late as 1630 in a meditation by Bishop Hall "on the sight of a blackamoor":

This is our colour spiritually; yet the eye of our gracious God and Saviour, can see that beauty in us wherewith he is delighted. The true Moses marries a Blackamoor; Christ, his church. It is not for us to regard the skin, but the soul. If that be innocent, pure, holy, the blots of an outside cannot set us off from the love of him who hath said, *Behold, thou art fair, my Sister, my Spouse:* if that be foul and black, it is not in the power of an angelical brightness of our hide, to make us other than a loathsome eye-sore to the Almighty.[15]

It is to this spiritual dynamic that Desdemona is clearly referring when she says, "I saw Othello's visage in his mind," and to which we ourselves are compelled to refer Othello once he comes on stage. His sense of command, of public decorum and courtesy, his dignity, and above all his remarkable devotion to Desdemona are instantly evident. The impression they make is all the more powerful, as Hunter and others have suggested, because Shakespeare has deliberately implicated us in the primordial prejudices of that other conception of the black man evoked in the first scene of the play. We ourselves thus experience, we do not merely witness, the process of perception Desdemona describes. That process is kept constantly in our consciousness by Othello's literal appearance, by the pervasive imagery of blackness and fairness and of true and false vision, and by Iago's increasingly ominous and explicitly diabolic threats to turn the spiritual metaphor into an "ocular proof." Under these circumstances, and given the concurrent development of Desdemona as an incarnate ideal of marital love and of the charity that subsumes it, Othello's marked worship of her is an expression not, as so many critics would have it, of the intrinsic weakness of his own love, but of its potential strength. Brabantio's last bitter words in the play are:

> Look to her, Moor, if thou hast eyes to see:
> She has deceiv'd her father, and may thee.

Othello answers, with an absolutism that characterizes him throughout, "My life upon her faith" (I. 3. 292-4). Iago is later to make deadly use of Brabantio's words, and when Othello immediately turns to "honest Iago" to care for Desdemona, we feel Othello's peril. His absolute commitment to Desdemona increases the peril, but it is not therefore in itself idolatrous. His investment in Desdemona's vision of him, as opposed to her father's, is a precisely Christian choice, the very reverse of idolatry. It is a manifestation of the faith that in Elizabethan eyes was the deepest resource of the love that unites a man and woman in marriage.

The discrepancy between Othello's and Desdemona's age has much the same effect as his blackness in the early acts and is similarly related to the reverence that marks his love for her. As several critics have observed,[16] the marriage of an old man and a young girl was traditional material for comedy or farce, but Shakespeare again inverts his audience's expectations and thereby intensifies its response. Desdemona, as we have seen, is no May. She loves Othello body and soul, unreservedly, and neither at the beginning nor at the tragic end of the marriage is she ever untrue to the ideal of one flesh to which she has consecrated herself. Othello, similarly, in the beginning, is no January. He is a general replete with power and respect, and unlike his comic prototypes, as Shakespeare takes pains to establish, he is neither lascivious nor impotent. In a much misunderstood speech to the Duke and Venetian lords, he seconds Desdemona's request to accompany him to Cyprus, "not," as he says,

> To please the palate of my appetite;
> Nor to comply with heat – the young affects
> In me defunct – and proper satisfaction;
> But to be free and bounteous to her mind.
> And heaven defend your good souls that you think
> I will your serious and great business scant
> For she is with me.

> (I. 3. 262)

Because of the crux in lines 263–4 the speech is not entirely clear, but there is no warrant, I think, for seeing a pathological sexual defensiveness in it. Desdemona's request, in wartime, is unusual, and Othello wants her to be with him at the same time that he wishes to assure the senators that they can rely on him to fulfill his office. So he points out, what we already have reason to accept, that he is a mature and moderate man, that he is not driven by appetite and heat, and that he knows how to value Desdemona for her companionship and spirit. At the same time, whatever the syntax, "the young affects" are those that are defunct, and there is no suggestion in the remainder of the speech that he does not expect or wish to consummate his marriage. His emphasis, in this highly public statement, is on the propriety of his behavior as a general as well as an older man.[17] Elizabethans would have had far more sympathy than we do with both concerns: they took the decorum of public life more seriously, and they did not idolize youth or its appetites. Later, on the first night in Cyprus, with the threat of war over, Othello explicitly invites his wife to bed in language that blends scriptural and physical allusiveness:

> Come, my dear love,
> The purchase made, the fruits are to ensue;
> The profit's yet to come 'twixt me and you.
>
> (II. 3. 8)

There is no question, except for those critics who would prefer the play to be hiding a novel within it, that the marriage is consummated. Nor is there any suggestion in the behavior of the two the morning after that the consummation has not been pleasurable.

The evocation of January and May, moreover, has a further purpose than simple inversion, for Shakespeare uses Othello's age, as he does his blackness, to dramatize the elemental composition of his marriage. As we have seen, the emphasis in the depiction of Othello's blackness is primarily, though by no means exclusively, religious; the deeper connotations of his age are developed in more psychological terms. January figures were commonly depicted in the second childhood of senility. Shakespeare, in his genius, appropriates the convention to give Othello much of the primal character of a child. A professional soldier, a stranger to Venetian culture and sophistication, and coming to marriage late in life, he seems innocent as well as vulnerable and, without depriving him of his actual manhood, Shakespeare endows him with many of the emotional responses and much of the peculiar vision of a very young boy. What Northrop Frye has described as the "curious quality in Othello's imagination that can only be called cosmological," and what G. Wilson Knight has discriminated in a different way as "The *Othello* Music" are both functions of that vision.[18] They both spring from the primal world of a child's feelings and fantasies, and Othello's habitation in that world is a potent source of his heroic energy throughout the play. In the early acts the accent is on a child's primitive capacity for wonder and worship, and it is demonstrated in Othello's "rude" speech as well as in the life history that he runs through for Brabantio,

> even from my boyish days
> To th' very moment that he bade me tell it;
> Wherein I spake of most disastrous chances,
> Of moving accidents by flood and field;
> Of hairbreadth scapes i' th' imminent deadly breach;
> Of being taken by the insolent foe
> And sold to slavery; of my redemption thence,
> And portance in my travel's history;
> Wherein of antres vast and deserts idle,
> Rough quarries, rocks, and hills whose heads touch heaven,
> It was my hint to speak – such was the process;
> And of the Cannibals that each other eat,
> The Anthropophagi, and men whose heads
> Do grow beneath their shoulders.
>
> (I. 3. 132)

Othello's capacity to generate wonder is ultimately an expression of his capacity to feel it, and it is his own childlike wonder and reverence that make his love for Desdemona in the early acts so remarkable. A child's first erotic relationship is with his mother, toward whom he develops intense feelings of affection and desire. Freud argued that a child initially experiences his mother and her nourishment as a virtual extension of himself: "We say that a human being has originally two sexual objects – himself and the woman who nurses him – and in doing so we are postulating a primary narcissism in everyone." In infancy both the mother and child experience a sense of symbiotic union, and that sense continues in a child's early development, as his "possession" of his mother and her love becomes an objectification of his most idealized vision of himself. Eventually, of course, with his father both an obstacle and a support, a boy surrenders much of his narcissism and learns to transfer his erotic feelings from himself and his mother to other women, but a man's image of his mother is never lost and, in his deepest and most complete sexual relationships, his early sense of union with his mother, "the primal condition in which object-libido and ego-libido cannot be distinguished," remains the model of sexual ecstasy and the source of his most passionate as well as exalted romantic feelings. Freud himself concluded that no marriage is secure "until the wife has succeeded in making her husband her child as well and in acting as a mother to him."[19]

Desdemona from first to last expresses these primal ideals in her love for Othello – a love that like a mother's is literally unconditional, though at the same time it is freely sexual, and at the beginning Othello responds to it with corresponding primal force. He invests his whole being in his love for her, and in the early acts he always speaks of and to her with that sense of symbiotic exaltation that is the remembrance of childhood, a sense that reaches its apogee in Cyprus, when they are reunited after their journey over "the enchafed flood":

> *Enter* OTHELLO *and* ATTENDANTS.
>
> OTHELLO: O my fair warrior!
> DESDEMONA:                 My dear Othello!
> OTHELLO: It gives me wonder great as my content
>     To see you here before me. O my soul's joy!
>     If after every tempest come such calms,
>     May the winds blow till they have waken'd death,
>     And let the labouring bark climb hills of seas
>     Olympus-high and duck again as low
>     As hell's from heaven. If it were now to die,
>     'Twere now to be most happy; for I fear
>     My soul hath her content so absolute
>     That not another comfort like to this
>     Succeeds in unknown fate.
> DESDEMONA:             The heavens forbid
>     But that our loves and comforts should increase
>     Even as our days do grow!
> OTHELLO:              Amen to that, sweet powers!
>     I cannot speak enough of this content;
>     It stops me here; it is too much of joy.
>     And this, and this, the greatest discords be [*They kiss.*]
>     That e'er our hearts shall make!
>
>                                  (II. 1. 180)

Freud observed, in discussing the love for which a man leaves father and mother to cleave to his wife, that "the greatest intensity of sensual passion will bring with it the highest mental estimation of the object (the normal over-estimation of the sexual object characteristic of men)." In a similar connection he wrote that "this sexual overvaluation is the origin of the peculiar state of being in love," and that its deepest impulse is to recapture the primary narcissism of childhood: "To be their own ideal once more, in regard to sexual no less than other trends, as they were in childhood – this is what people strive to attain as their happiness."[20] Freud's discussion of narcissism suggests perhaps an underlying psychological reason for the prominence of images of mirrors in medieval and Renaissance erotic literature.[21] It is also closely analogous to the biblical theme of the regaining of Eden, "a world of original identity," and in art, as Northrop Frye has pointed out, the theme frequently takes the form of a "return . . . not to childhood but to a state of innocence symbolized by childhood." Frye remarks also that in romance literature "the traditional symbolic basis of the sexual quest, which goes back to the Song of Songs in the Bible, is the identification of the mistress' body with the paradisal garden."[22]

The association of Desdemona with such symbolism is particularly strong in *Othello* (and accounts in part for Shakespeare's great insistence on her innocence), and Othello's reunion with her on Cyprus, the most ecstatic moment of the play, draws deeply on the primal psychological and religious sources of all erotic yearning. The movement of desire and feeling in *Othello* expresses precisely the state of being in love that Freud describes, and the whole of the scene is infused with visual and verbal hyperboles of erotic exaltation. G. Wilson Knight writes that in this scene Othello is "essential man," Desdemona "essential woman," and that "here especially Othello appears a prince of heroes, Desdemona is lit by a divine feminine radiance: both are transfigured."[23] I think that Knight does not exaggerate. The scene is incandescent, and any interpretation that ignores its primal beauty and power is substituting a different play for the one Shakespeare wrote. It is true that as Othello speaks, with Iago as witness, we recognize his vulnerability, and we may also find tremors of anxiety in what he says but, given that very vulnerability, his anxiety is justified and functions in this scene as a measure of the extraordinary intensity of his hope and of his love. Iago, unlike his modern critical affiliates, does not mistake the beauty of what he sees:

> O, you are well tun'd now!
> But I'll set down the pegs that make this music,
> As honest as I am.
>
> (II. 1. 197)

Iago, of course, succeeds in his malevolent quest, and there can be no question that he does so, in part, as F. R. Leavis has insisted, because ''he represents something that is in Othello – in Othello the husband of Desdemona: the essential traitor is within the gates.'' Leavis's conclusion that Othello's love is therefore a pretense and that the play boils down to a study of ''an obtuse and brutal egotism'' seems to me not to follow and indeed to exhibit a superficial understanding of the nature both of egotism and tragedy, but I think his initial perception is undeniable.[24] Shakespeare suggests in the simplest mechanics of the opening dialogue of the temptation scene, through Iago's insistent echoing of Othello's own words, that the process we are to witness is fundamentally an internal one:

IAGO: My noble lord!
OTHELLO:                    What dost thou say, Iago?
IAGO: Did Michael Cassio, when you woo'd my lady,
       Know of your love?
OTHELLO: He did, from first to last. Why dost thou ask?
IAGO: But for a satisfaction of my thought –
       No further harm.
OTHELLO:                    Why of thy thought, Iago?
IAGO: I did not think he had been acquainted with her.
OTHELLO: O, yes: and went between us very often.
IAGO: Indeed!
OTHELLO: Indeed? Ay, indeed. Discern'st thou aught in that?
       Is he not honest?

IAGO:                        Honest, my lord?
OTHELLO: Honest? Ay, honest.
IAGO:                        My lord, for aught I know.
OTHELLO: What dost thou think?
IAGO:                        Think, my lord?
OTHELLO: Think, my lord! By heaven, he echoes me,
          As if there were some monster in his thought
          Too hideous to be shown.

                                              (III. 3. 94)

Iago's words, in this exchange, literally emanate from Othello. Iago is certainly the aggressor, but Othello is clearly ready to respond, and it is he who actively makes the association between the words Iago repeats and the threatening thought behind them. It is he who introduces the pregnant words "honest" and "think," and it is he, as well as Iago, who creates the monstrous collocation between the two. The dialogue thus schematically implies what the remainder of the temptation scene and the play demonstrates, that Iago echoes something within Othello, that he is a projection of at least a part of Othello's own psyche.

Iago's psychomachic role would have been unmistakable to Elizabethans. Bernard Spivack has argued, in a now familiar book,[25] that most of Iago's salient stage characteristics are drawn from the figure of the Vice in medieval and Tudor drama: his stage-managing, his artistry in evil that Bradley was the first to emphasize, his aggression through deceit, his corruption of the word, his persistent asides, his intimate relationship with the audience, his vaudevillian gusto, and above all his apparent motivelessness except for the instinct to destroy: all these features were conventional attributes of the Vice. More recent, and I think persuasive, scholarship has suggested, as Othello does when he looks down at Iago's feet at the end of the play, that he is more akin to the devil, and there is considerable evidence that devils and Vices had similar theatrical characteristics.[26] The distinction is not a small one, because as a Vice, Iago would be an allegorical expression purely of Othello's own inner disposition to viciousness, whereas as the devil, he dramatizes a temptation to evil that exists both without and within Othello. The difference is most important to our response to the play and I shall return to it, but for the moment we should recognize that in either case Iago represents as deep a wellspring in Othello's soul as Desdemona does and carries as great a religious and psychological resonance.

The theological dynamics of Iago's usurpation of Desdemona's place in Othello's being is quite explicit, and its essential locus is once again Othello's (and Desdemona's) color. Iago repeatedly associates his diabolic auspices with the capacity to invert darkness and light:

> Hell and night
> Must bring this monstrous birth to the world's light.
>
> (I. 3. 397)

> Divinity of hell!
> When devils will their blackest sins put on,
> They do suggest at first with heavenly shows,
> As I do now.
>
> (II. 3. 339)

It is at the end of the latter speech that he promises to turn Desdemona's "virtue into pitch," and he fulfils that promise, ultimately, because he succeeds in making Othello believe only in the letter of his own blackness. When Brabantio first taunts Othello to look to Desdemona if he has "eyes to see," Othello answers, as we have seen, with a testimony of faith that is subsumed by Desdemona's vision of him, "I saw Othello's visage in his mind." Midway in the temptation scene, however, once Iago's thoughts, and his own, have begun to take effect, he tells Iago:

> Nor from mine own weak merits will I draw
> The smallest fear or doubt of her revolt;
> For she had eyes, and chose me. No, Iago;
> I'll see before I doubt; when I doubt, prove;
> And, on the proof, there is no more but this –
> Away at once with love or jealousy!
>
> (III. 3. 191)

This speech is the immediate prelude to his fall, as well as the
predication of it, for once he accepts the epistemology of "normal" Venetian eyesight, he is doomed. After reminding him
that Desdemona, "so young, could give out such a seeming, / To
seel her father's eyes up close as oak" (III. 3. 213), Iago can
thereafter easily persuade him that there must be something
monstrous in Desdemona's love for him, and it is an inevitable
step to the conclusion that

> Her name, that was as fresh
> As Dian's visage, is now begrim'd and black
> As mine own face.
>
> (III. 3. 390)

It is no exaggeration to suggest, given the pervasive spiritual
connotations of blackness in the play, that at this point Othello
has lost his faith and is in a state of despair. The Godlike pre-
sumption that masks his subsequent vengeance ("This sorrow's
heavenly; / It strikes where it doth love" [V. 2. 21]) only confirms
that inner state, as does his increasing incapacity to accept or
believe in Desdemona's love. His eventual destruction of her is
itself an irremissable, suicidal act. He has loved her as his own
flesh, and when he destroys her he destroys himself. And he
knows it.

The psychoanalytical ramifications of Iago's aggression
against Othello, which is to say, Othello's unconscious aggression against himself, are equally profound and are consonant
with the theological overtones. Iago is Desdemona's sexual as
well as spiritual antagonist. Where she luminously represents a
union of affection and desire, Iago wishes to reduce love
"merely" to "a lust of the blood and a permission of the will" (I.
3. 333). He repeatedly assures Roderigo that the love of Desdemona and Othello cannot last, that by its very nature it must
fail:

The food that to him now is as luscious as locusts shall be to him shortly
as acerbe as the coloquintida. She must change for youth; when she is
sated with his body, she will find the error of her choice.

> (I. 3. 350)

Mark me with what violence she first lov'd the Moor, but for bragging and telling her fantastical lies. To love him still for prating? – let not thy discreet heart think it. Her eye must be fed; and what delight shall she have to look on the devil? When the blood is made dull with the act of sport, there should be – again to inflame it, and to give satiety a fresh appetite – loveliness in favour, sympathy in years, manners, and beauties – all which the Moor is defective in. Now for want of these requir'd conveniences, her delicate tenderness will find itself abus'd, begin to heave the gorge, disrelish and abhor the Moor; very nature will instruct her in it, and compel her to some second choice.

(II. 1. 219)

Considering the number of critics who, like Auden, end up agreeing with Iago's assumptions, it should be noted that Iago is speaking to Roderigo, the simplest of gulls (and even he objects), and speaking disingenuously. As Iago's soliloquies show, his deepest animus against Othello and Desdemona stems precisely from his belief that their "free and open nature" makes them capable of proving him wrong. The basic motive of his malignancy, like Satan's, is envy.

Iago nevertheless prevails with Othello, as I have already suggested, because Othello eventually internalizes Iago's maleficent sexual vision and sees himself with Iago's eyes, rather than Desdemona's; and again the core of his vulnerability, as of his romantic distinction, is his age and color. At a critical turn in the argument of the temptation scene, Othello wonders that "nature" should be "erring from itself" in Desdemona (III. 3. 231). It is a line that could be construed and meant as a protest against Iago's insinuations, but Iago quickly transforms it into a deeply subversive sexual indictment:

Ay, there's the point: as – to be bold with you –
Not to affect many proposed matches
Of her own clime, complexion, and degree,
Whereto we see in all things nature tends –
Foh! one may smell in such a will most rank,
Foul disproportion, thoughts unnatural.

(III. 3. 232)

Shortly afterwards, Othello adopts those thoughts as his own, and explicitly associates them with his color and his age:

> Haply, for I am black
> And have not those soft parts of conversation
> That chamberers have, or for I am declin'd
> Into the vale of years – yet that's not much –
> She's gone; I am abus'd; and my relief
> Must be to loathe her. O curse of marriage,
> That we can call these delicate creatures ours,
> And not their appetites!

(III. 3. 267)

This is the crux of Othello's fall, and his union with Iago's world of blood lust follows immediately. He believes that Desdemona cannot be true because he becomes convinced that he himself is unlovable and, believing that, he also becomes convinced that Desdemona's manifest attraction to him is itself perverse, a "proof" of her corruption. Just before he strangles her, he and she have the following acutely painful dialogue:

OTHELLO: Think on thy sins.
DESDEMONA:                    They are loves I bear to you.
OTHELLO: Ay, and for that thou diest.
DESDEMONA: That death's unnatural that kills for loving.

(V. 2. 43)

I am not altogether sure what these lines mean. Desdemona may be referring to the sin of disobeying her father. Othello may be condemning Desdemona for her very desire for him, or he may be projecting upon her his incapacity to accept his own desires, probably both. And hovering over the lines may be the sense of guilt of the original sin, which was at once physical and spiritual. But whatever their precise meaning, the lines convey the ultimate horror of the play, which is Othello's radical rejection of the precept upon which his, or any, marriage is founded: "So men are bound to love their own wives as their own bodies. He that loveth his own wife, loveth himself." The tragedy of Othello is that finally he fails to love his own body, to love himself, and it is this despairing self-hatred that spawns the enormous savagery, degradation, and destructiveness of his jealousy.

The awesome energy of Othello's jealousy, its primitive and superstitious vindictiveness, is a function of the same primal forces that animated his earlier exaltation and love. As a child matures, he must inevitably be separated from his mother, he must confront the reality first that she is not a part of him and then that she has a sexual love for his father from which he is obviously and necessarily excluded. In the Freudian cosmology this conflict is inescapable, and the child, before he experiences his inevitable Oedipal defeat and learns to reconstitute himself, experiences profound feelings of betrayal, and rivalry, and rage, and threats of the loss of identity and of nurture. It is this constellation of feelings that is the primal source of sexual jealousy and that is tapped directly in the second half of *Othello:*

> alas, to make me
> The fixed figure for the time of scorn
> To point his slow unmoving finger at! – O, O!
> Yet could I bear that too; well, very well;
> But there, where I have garner'd up my heart,
> Where either I must live or bear no life,
> The fountain from the which my current runs,
> Or else dries up – to be discarded thence!
> Or keep it as a cistern for foul toads
> To knot and gender in! Turn thy complexion there,
> Patience, thou young and rose-lipp'd cherubin –
> Ay, here, look grim as hell.
>
> (IV. 2. 54)

This is not a pleasant passage to contemplate, but it is very important to an understanding of the play, for its conflation of images of the breast and of the womb expresses the precise etiology of Othello's jealous anguish and suggests the tragic vulnerability of a love so absolutely rooted in, and dependent upon, the exaltation of symbiotic union.

A similar condensation of imagery accumulates around the handkerchief, the accidental hinge of the plot whose "triviality" has so bedevilled the play's critics from Rymer onwards. "That handkerchief," Othello first explains,

> Did an Egyptian to my mother give.
> She was a charmer, and could almost read
> The thoughts of people; she told her, while she kept it,
> 'Twould make her amiable, and subdue my father
> Entirely to her love; but if she lost it,
> Or made a gift of it, my father's eye
> Should hold her loathely, and his spirits should hunt
> After new fancies.

(III. 4. 55)

The superstitious cast of this speech is a regression not merely to Othello's literally primitive past, but to the primitive world of a child's merger with his mother, and there is already implicit in what Othello says the sense of his own primal betrayal. It is not then essentially an accident that the handkerchief should become coextensive in his mind with his jealous fantasy of Desdemona's actual betrayal of him and with his thoughts of revenge:

Lie with her – lie on her? We say lie on her when they belie her. Lie with her. Zounds, that's fulsome. Handkerchief – confessions – handkerchief! To confess, and be hang'd for his labour – first, to be hang'd, and then to confess. I tremble at it. Nature would not invest herself in such shadowing passion without some instruction. It is not words that shakes me thus – pish! – noses, ears, and lips. Is't possible? Confess! Handkerchief! O devil! [Falls in a trance.]

(IV. I. 34)

What has clearly become insupportable for Othello in this scene is the fulsomeness of his own sexual instincts and, as his verbal and physical decomposition suggests, his jealous rage against Cassio is ultimately a rage against himself that reaches back to the elemental and destructive triadic fantasies that at one stage in childhood govern the mind of every human being.

In the broadest sense, Othello's behavior in the second half of the play is a dramatization of guilt. In Christian terms the temptation scene recollects the Fall of Man, which Augustine interpreted as an allegorical representation of an essentially psychomachic process, the disorder of the soul by which reason becomes subjected to passion. In analogous psychoanalytic terms, the guilt is the aggression of the unconscious, again an internal process, in which Iago represents one part of Othello and Desdemona another, and in which his destruction of Desdemona is a literal enactment of his ultimately self-destructive aggression against himself. I do not think it follows, however, as most theological and psychological critics seem to believe, that the play is therefore throughout or essentially a pathological study either of an idolator or a narcissist, however many attributes of both Othello may in fact demonstrate. It seems to me, on the contrary, that such approaches profoundly misconstrue, where they do not utterly ignore, the play's actual experience.

To begin with, and one cannot overemphasize the point, Desdemona is as much a part of Othello's soul, whether spiritually or psychically conceived, as Iago. She is not a fantasy, or rather she is a fantasy made flesh: the life, not only the imago, of that union of tenderness and desire, that unconditional love, toward which all men aspire. And Othello marries her, the whole first half of the play celebrates his incandescent erotic feelings for her, and in the second half his torment and decomposition can be measured, as they always are in his own consciousness, by his loss of her. It is deeply fitting in his final speech, and cheering to us if not to him, that his dying recognition that she was true should enable him genuinely to recover a sense of his former being, just as his delusion that she was faithless had caused him to lose it.[27]

Correspondingly, Iago does not constitute the whole of Othello's spiritual state or of his unconscious. He is not simply a projection of Othello's own disposition to vice, though he of course plays upon it. He is not a Vice but, as he himself repeatedly announces and everyone else in the play eventually recognizes, a "hellish villain" (V. 2. 371). He is the eternal tempter who succeeds because he attacks in Othello not just his frailty but the frailty of all men. Auden suggested, astutely, that Iago "treats Othello as an analyst treats a patient except that, of course, his intention is to kill not to cure." Auden went on to observe that everything Iago says "is designed to bring to Othello's consciousness what he has already guessed is there";[28] but a further and crucial point should be made, which is that what is "there" exists as part of the unconscious life of all men. It is not peculiar to Othello, though it is tragically heightened in him. The issue is not an abstract one in *Othello*, because within the world that Shakespeare creates in the play honest Iago is a spokesman for what everyone else, save Desdemona, feels or believes or represents. Othello's guilt, in fact, pervades his society, and Iago has only to return to him the image of himself that he can see reflected, not in fantasy but in reality, in the world about him. Brabantio, who was formerly his friend, who "lov'd" and "oft invited" him to his house, vilifies him and believes that Desdemona is bewitched and that the marriage is obscene; and, as we have observed, the opening of the play implicates us as well as Venetian society in this deep racial prejudice. Cassio idolizes Desdemona and at the same time is capable of a sexual relationship only with a whore of whom he is essentially contemptuous. And in a proleptic version of Othello's fall, he gets drunk and violent on Othello's wedding night. The only other marriage in the play is Iago's and Emilia's, and although Emilia's portrayal is very complex it is nevertheless obvious that Iago has little affection for her and that at least the premises of her own worldly realism are not far from his. Only at the end, in a response to Desdemona's fidelity, which neither she nor certainly Iago would ever have anticipated, does she move into another realm of feeling and value; and even then she finds Desdemona's marriage incomprehensible, if not repellent: "She was too fond of her most filthy bargain" (V. 2. 160). The "proper" Lodovico, to be sure, floats into view at the end of the play as a hypothetical husband, but he is a visitor to the play's tragic experience, like Fortinbras in *Hamlet,* not a part of it; he picks up the pieces at the end. It is no wonder that Othello, literally an alien by his profession, his background, his color, and his age, should in such a world find it tragically impossible to hold to the scriptural belief, which is also Desdemona's, that he is "black, but beautiful." Freud remarked in *Civilization and Its Discontents* that "in an individual neurosis we take as our starting-point the contrast that distinguishes the patient from his environment, which is assumed to be 'normal.'"[29] No such assumption can be made about the environment of *Othello*, either in Venice or Cyprus. It is not normal, it is itself guilt-ridden, and Othello is at once its victim and its heroic sacrifice.

In a tragic universe, it is worth stressing, guilt is inescapable; and the hero commands our minds and hearts not because he is sick or healthy, saved or damned, but because he most deeply incarnates and experiences the inexorable tragic conditions that we recognize in our own existence. In *Othello* those tragic conditions are explicitly sexual, whether they are understood in religious or psychological terms, and from an Elizabethan or modern perspective. Freud's own view, expressed consistently in his writing, was that the Oedipal drama that forms the basis of all human sexual development is fundamentally tragic. In the essay from which I quoted at the start of this discussion, "The Most Prevalent Form of Degradation in Erotic Life," he argued that the dissociation of affection and sensuality that characterizes cases of actual psychical impotence is in the last analysis a condition of all human beings; that the two currents of erotic feeling, "the same two that are personified in art as heavenly and earthly (or animal) love," are rarely completely fused in civilized man. He remarked:

It has an ugly sound and a paradoxical as well, but nevertheless it must be said that whoever is to be really free and happy in love must have overcome his deference for women and come to terms with the idea of incest with mother or sister. Anyone who in the face of this test subjects himself to serious self-examination will indubitably find that at the bottom of his heart he too regards the sexual act as something degrading, which soils and contaminates not only the body.[30]

Freud concluded that "however strange it may sound, I think the possibility must be considered that something in the nature of the sexual instinct itself is unfavourable to the achievement of absolute gratification." The whole of this essay is the nucleus of Freud's later, more celebrated, discussion of aggression and guilt in *Civilization and Its Discontents*.

Freud, of course, did not originate these ideas. Similar concepts are inherent and often developed in a considerable body of medieval and Renaissance literature combining erotic and theological themes, and in his own time Shakespeare would have found them stated with Freudian explicitness in Montaigne's "Upon Some Verses of *Virgil*," the essay from which he almost certainly drew directly in *All's Well That Ends Well*. Because Montaigne himself actually tended to degrade women, he illustrates Freud's thought as well as parallels it. His essay deals with sexuality, and a large part of it constitutes an argument against the possibility of uniting the affection that belongs to marriage and the *"insatiate thirst of enjoying a greedily desired subject"* that belongs to sensual love:

*Love disdaineth a man should hold of other then himselfe,* and dealeth but faintly with acquaintances begun and entertained under another title; as mariage is. . . . Nor is it other than a kinde of incest, in this reverent alliance and sacred bond, to employ the efforts and extravagant humor of an amorous licentiousness. . . . Wedlocke hath for his share honour, justice, profit and constancie: a plaine, but more generall delight. Love melts in onely pleasure.

Like Freud, Montaigne finds something paradoxically degrading about the very "acte of generation":

In al other things you may observe decorum and maintaine some decency: all other operations admit some rules of honesty: this cannot onely be imagined, but vicious or ridiculous. . . . Surely it is an argument not onely of our originall corruption, but a badge of our vanity and deformity. On the one side nature urgeth us unto it: having thereunto combined, yea fastned, the most noble, the most profitable, and the most sensually-pleasing, of all her functions: and on the other suffereth us to accuse, to condemne and to shunne it, as insolent, as dishonest, and as lewder to blush at it, and allow, yea and to command abstinence. *Are not we most brutish, to terme that worke beastly which begets, and which maketh us?*

Montaigne, like Freud, observes the ultimate incapacity of erotic instincts to be fully satisfied or harmonized

> But withall *it is against the nature of love, not to be violent, and against the condition of violence, to be constant....* It is not a passion meerely corporeall. *If no end be found in coveteousness, nor limit in ambition, assure your selfe there is nor end nor limit in letchery.* It yet continueth after saciety: nor can any man prescribe it or end or constant satisfaction: it ever goeth on beyond it's possession, beyond it's bounds.

Montaigne says finally of marriage that "It is a match whereto may well be applied the common saying, *homo homini aut Deus, aut Lupus ... Man unto man is either a God or a Wolfe.*"[31]

It is within this polarized erotic universe that Othello moves, and he traverses its extremes not only in the larger parabolic action of his marriage and its destruction, but in the very constitution of his being. At the exact hinge of the play's action, just after Desdemona leaves him with her plea for Cassio, and the instant before Iago begins his attack, Othello says,

> Excellent wretch! Perdition catch my soul
> But I do love thee; and when I love thee not,
> Chaos is come again.
>
> (III. 3. 91)

These well-known lines spring from the heart of Othello's existence and describe the essence of the paradox that at once animates and destroys him. At the end, in his last words, I think he speaks the basic truth, both of his experience and of our response to it, when he says that he is "one that lov'd not wisely, but too well" (V. 2. 347). The play has deep affiliations with romance. It is a full and moving anatomy of love, not a clinical diagnosis or demonstration, and Othello is its hero not because he achieves triumph or suffers defeat, though he does both, nor because he learns or does not learn a theological or psychological lesson, but because he is indeed, as Cassio says, "great of heart," and because he enacts for us, with beautiful and terrifying nakedness, the primitive energies that are the substance of our own erotic lives.

# 3

# Much Ado About Nothing

The harmony that characterizes almost all performances of *Much Ado About Nothing* is very difficult to capture in criticism. On stage the play has unfailing comic integrity and poise, but its unity is elusive, and many critics are inclined actually to dissociate its plots and to attribute its sense of theatrical coherence and power solely to the comic feast of language in the characterizations of Dogberry, Beatrice, and Benedick, the three roles that invariably dominate a performance.

This was George Bernard Shaw's approach, and his analysis of the play, though perverse, is instructive. He attacks the "pretension in *Much Ado* . . . that Benedick and Beatrice are exquisitely witty and amusing persons." He argues that Benedick, like many of Shakespeare's "merry gentlemen" seems to have only one thing on his mind: "From his first joke, 'Were you in doubt, sir, that you asked her?' to his last, 'There is no staff more reverend than one tipped with horn,' he is not a wit, but a blackguard." Benedick's celebrated wit, Shaw insists, is composed primarily of "coarse sallies," "indecent jests," "lewdness," "obscenity," and even "brutality." "Precisely the same thing," he continues,

in the tenderer degree of her sex, is true of Beatrice. In her character of professed wit she has only one subject, and that is the subject which a really witty woman never jests about, because it is too serious a matter to a woman to be made light of without indelicacy. Beatrice jests about it for the sake of indelicacy. There is only one thing worse than the Elizabethan 'merry gentleman,' and that is the Elizabethan 'merry lady.'[1]

Why, then, Shaw asks, should we still want to see Benedick
and Beatrice on stage and our most eminent actors and actresses
still want to play them? His answer is that the language of their
jokes stands in the same relation to their content as Mozart's
music in *Don Giovanni* does to the "loathsome story" of the
libretto. The opera is immortal

> simply because Mozart clothed it with wonderful music, which turned
> the worthless words and thoughts of Da Porte into a magical human
> drama of moods and transitions of feeling. That is what happened in a
> smaller way with *Much Ado*. Shakespear shews himself in it a com-
> monplace librettist working on a stolen plot, but a great musician. No
> matter how poor, coarse, cheap, and obvious the thought may be, the
> mood is charming, and the music of the words expresses the mood.
> Paraphrase the encounters of Benedick and Beatrice in the style of a
> bluebook, carefully preserving every idea they present, and it will be-
> come apparent to the most infatuated Shakespearean that they contain
> at best nothing out of the common in thought or wit and at worst a
> good deal of vulgar naughtiness.[2]

Shaw's own jokes, of course, could hardly stand such a test –
no joke can – but his attitudes are nonetheless symptomatic of a
great deal of contemporary criticism of *Much Ado*. Most critics
would not now share his sexual prudery or agree with his parallel between Shakespeare and Da Ponte, but few, I think, would
object to his distinction between the play's ideas and its theatrical effect. Modern critics usually praise the play's freedom from
ideology, but they thereby invert Shaw's opposition, they do
not change it. For the majority of recent critics, as for Shaw,
*Much Ado About Nothing* is an enjoyable but essentially empty
play.

It seems to me that this dichotomy is unfortunate, not only
because it reduces criticism of the play to increasingly arid ob-
servations about technique, but because it is so clearly false to
the theatrical experience it purports to describe, an experience
that is rich not only in laughter, but also in the deeper processes
of thought and feeling upon which laughter depends. The heart
of *Much Ado* is indeed its comic energy, which ranges dialectically from the naiveté of Dogberry to the hypersophistication of

Beatrice and Benedick, but that energy is itself organically related to the serious issues and feelings generated by the story of
Claudio and Hero. Shaw is obviously correct, for example, in
noting Benedick's and Beatrice's manifest preoccupation with
sexuality, and there is little doubt also that part of the pleasure
we take in them is operatic, but Shaw misses the essential point,
which is that they are comically compelling precisely because
they themselves understand, and the play as a whole supports,
the significance of what they appear to make light of. They joke
most, both of them, about what the action of *Much Ado*, as well
as their own instincts and intelligence, demonstrates is most
fundamental to the relation between men and women. Their
jests are usually conventional, about cuckolds and horns, about
men who are unmanly and women who are untrue, but the
conventions themselves acquire a special urgency in the play,
for them and for us, because the fears and fantasies that inform
their jests are in fact acted out in the courtship of Claudio and
Hero, and through that courtship sharply focused upon both the
spiritual and psychological implications of love and marriage.
The same implications are enacted, less obviously but even more
profoundly, by the comedy of Dogberry and the Watch. As I
suggested previously, the three plots of the play are entirely
interdependent, nourishing each other by continuous analogies
of action and language, and no one of them can be understood
in isolation from the others.

At the center of all three is the scene in which Claudio carries
out his promise to shame Hero, a scene whose original object, in
the words of the *Book of Common Prayer*, is the "forme and sol-
emnization of Matrimony." Claudio initially delays making his
accusations. The Friar is asked to celebrate "the plain form of
marriage" and both he and Claudio solemnly echo the liturgy,
the Friar by charging the couple on their "souls" to "utter" their
knowledge of any "inward impediment" to their marriage, and
Claudio by asking Leonato if he gives away his daughter with
"free and unconstrained soul" (IV. 1. 2, 11–14, 23). It is only then
that Claudio accuses Hero and the ceremony is aborted. The

scene thus concentrates our attention, both visually and intellectually, on a marriage ceremony. There is no other scene like it in Shakespeare's canon, and within the play itself its prominence is unmistakable. Almost all the early action of *Much Ado* moves directly toward it, and the subsequent action is devoted to its clarification and eventual fulfillment. It provides the context in which Benedick and Beatrice come together, resolving their own inward impediments and declaring their love, and it forms the focus of the whole comedy of Dogberry and the Watch.

The specific ceremony the scene evokes is still widely used, but its very familiarity has tended to drain it of meaning. The words of the liturgy, as well as the assumptions behind them, are worth rehearsing:

Dearly beloved friends, we are gathered together here in the sight of God, and in the face of his congregation, to join together this man and this woman in holy matrimony, which is an honorable estate, instituted of God in paradise in the time of man's innocency, signifying unto us the mystical union, that is betwixt Christ and his Church: which holy estate Christ adorned and beautified with his presence and first miracle that he wrought in Cana of Galilee, and is commended of Saint Paul to be honorable among all men, and therefore is not to be enterprised nor taken in hand unadvisedly, lightly, or wantonly, to satisfy men's carnal lusts and appetites, like brute beasts that have no understanding, but reverently, discreetly, advisedly, soberly, and in the fear of God, duly considering the causes for which matrimony was ordained. One was, the procreation of children to be brought up in the fear and nurture of the Lord, and praise of God. Secondly, it was ordained for a remedy against sin, and to avoid fornication, that such persons as have not the gift of continency might marry, and keep themselves undefiled members of Christ's body. Thirdly, for the mutual society, help, and comfort, that the one ought to have of the other, both in prosperity and adversity: into the which holy estate these two persons present come now to be joined. Therefore, if any man can show any just cause why they may not lawfully be joined together, let him now speak, or else hereafter forever hold his peace.

The priest then advises the persons to be married "that if either of you do know any impediment why ye may not be lawfully joined together in matrimony, that ye confess it." The service continues with the giving away of the bride, the plighting of troths, the recitation of either Psalm 128 or 67, and a number of prayers. It concludes with several scriptural teachings on the duties of marriage, one of them the passage from St. Paul that enjoins men "to love their own wives as their own bodies." Another citation of the Scripture, from 1 Peter, gives corresponding instruction to wives, including the prescription that they not let their "apparel... be outward, with broided hair and trimming about with gold, either in putting on of gorgeous apparel, but let the hid man which is in the heart, be without all corruption, so that the spirit be mild and quiet, which is a precious thing in the sight of God."[3]

The relevance of this ceremony to the church scene in *Much Ado* is obvious. Claudio accuses Hero not only of an act that marriage is specifically ordained to avoid, but of a spiritual and psychological condition in which true marriage is impossible. Claudio's words are closely related to the opening of the liturgy: He accuses Hero of the "semblance" of "honour," of "cunning sin," of being "an approved wanton" to whom he will not "knit" his "soul," of being "more intemperate" in her "blood / Than Venus, or those pamp'red animals / That rage in savage sensuality" (IV. 1. 32, 35, 43, 58–60). He accuses Hero, in short, of sin and faithlessness – of the blush of "guiltiness, not modesty," of "pure impiety and impious purity" (IV. 1. 41, 103).

Though Claudio has apparent provocation for these tortured oxymorons, we ourselves know that they do not apply to Hero; and I think we eventually also understand that they constitute an expression of feelings and impulses that are repressed within himself. He is, to be sure, presented as a conventional young and idealistic lover, but the idealism itself is questioned. Idealization, as Freud argued, is a normal expression of the narcissism that is at the root of love, because a lover tends to treat an object of love "in the same way as [his] own ego," but as Freud also noted, "If the sensual impulsions are more or less effectively repressed or set aside, the illusion is produced that the object has come to be sensually loved on account of its spiritual merits, whereas on the contrary these merits may really only have been lent to it by its sensual charm."⁴ Such an illusion seems to be at the root of Claudio's behavior. The heated carnal fantasies that emerge in his charges against Hero suggest the repression of his own sensuality, and his idealistic interest in her tends from the start to be overly self-centered. The terms of the speech in which he declares his love for her to Don Pedro are romantic, but he can actually apprehend her only as a possession (Benedick suggests as much when he asks him if he wishes to "buy" her [I. 1. 154]), and his repressed sensuality, the underside of his sentimentalism, is what persuades him that Don Pedro must have betrayed him, just as it later persuades him that Hero has:

> 'Tis certain so: the Prince woos for himself
> Friendship is constant in all other things
> Save in the office and affairs of love;
> Therefore all hearts in love use their own tongues.
> Let every eye negotiate for itself,
> And trust no agent: for beauty is a witch
> Against whose charms faith melteth into blood.
> This is an accident of hourly proof,
> Which I mistrusted not.
>
> (II. 1. 153)

Claudio's thinking here resembles Iago's, and the speech as a whole outlines the same psychological and moral pattern Shakespeare developed tragically in the later play. The emphasis upon the evidence – and credulity – of the eye and ear, the inversion of trust, and the suggestion even of witchcraft all anticipate major motifs in *Othello*. "Faith melteth into blood" could be the epigraph of the later play, and Claudio's whole characterization looks forward to Othello's. They have a similar narcissistic orientation, a similar vulnerability to diabolically slanderous suggestion, and above all, a similar polarization of romantic and sexual imaginings.

Claudio's psychology, however, is not developed in *Much Ado* – indeed his characterization is largely muted – and the serious psychic and spiritual consequences of his predicament, which in the later play are tragically focused in the hero, in *Much Ado* are diffused and refracted in the comic action of the play as a whole. Shakespeare represents Claudio as a victim not merely of slander but of his own unconscious disposition to believe it. By denying his senses, he becomes their virtual prisoner, believing only in what he sees and hears, repeatedly misled and repeatedly duped, a man who sees the outward apparel rather than the hid man that is in the heart. But he is not alone in that condition. Everyone in the play, except the villains and the Watchmen, hears or sees wrongly, everyone is vulnerable to slanderous suggestion, and everyone, though in varying degrees, is willing or disposed to believe that faith melts into blood. Intelligent and alert as they are, even Benedick and Beatrice can be fooled, and both are obviously apprehensive about marriage. Don Pedro, who is *Much Ado*'s social leader if not its monarch, is as susceptible to Don John's plot as Claudio is, and even Hero's own father finds it difficult to sustain his faith in her. In fact, the tendentious misinterpretation of sexual appearances that constitutes a primary mode of slander is also the mode of the play. The action of *Much Ado* is particularly marked by conversations that are wrongly heard or overheard and by sights that are mistakenly perceived. The play implies that such misapprehensions represent a spiritual and psychological, as well as a social, condition; virtually all the characters in the play at one point or another nurse wounds to their self-esteem and are radically self-absorbed. Don John, in his total self-conceit, is the sinister paradigm of this condition, as Dogberry is the beneficent one. *Much Ado* undoubtedly celebrates the manners of a civilized society, but it also represents, and deeply, the narcissistic "impediments" that make the achievement of such a community at once so difficult and so urgent.

The theological implications of these impediments are adumbrated with unusual emphasis in *Much Ado* in the remarkable dialogue between Borachio and Conrade about the plot against

Claudio and Hero – the dialogue that is overheard by the Watch and that eventually leads to Don John's exposure.

BORACHIO: Thou knowest that the fashion of a doublet, or a hat, or a cloak, is nothing to a man.

CONRADE: Yes, it is apparel.

BORACHIO: I mean the fashion.

CONRADE: Yes, the fashion is the fashion.

BORACHIO: Tush, I may as well say the fool's the fool. But seest thou not what a deformed thief this fashion is?

2 WATCH: [*Aside*] I know that Deformed; 'a has been a vile thief this seven year; 'a goes up and down like a gentleman; I remember his name.

BORACHIO: Didst thou not hear somebody?

CONRADE: No; 'twas the vane on the house.

BORACHIO: Seest thou not, I say, what a deformed thief this fashion is, how giddily 'a turns about all the hot bloods between fourteen and five and thirty, sometimes fashioning them like Pharoah's soldiers in the reechy painting, sometime like god Bel's priests in the old church-window, sometime like the shaven Hercules in the smirch'd worm-eaten tapestry, where his codpiece seems as massy as his club?

CONRADE: All this I see; and I see that the fashion wears out more apparel than the man. But art not thou thyself giddy with the fashion too, that thou hast shifted out of thy tale into telling me of the fashion?

BORACHIO: Not so neither; but know that I have to-night wooed Margaret, the Lady Hero's gentlewoman, by the name of Hero. . . .

(III. 3. 108)

Borachio then proceeds to inform Conrade of the details of his deception of Claudio and Don Pedro.

The intrusiveness of Borachio's homily is an indication of the pressure of thought behind it, and we should take him at his word when he insists that he has not shifted out of his tale. His discussion of fashion is a prelude to his revelation of the plot against Claudio and Hero and clearly suggests a spiritual context in which that plot, and consequently the main action of the play, may be understood. Claudio, who is associated with apparel and fashion throughout the play and who has, as we have seen, the play's most hot-blooded fantasies, is specifically implicated; but Borachio's references to the Pharoah's soldiers, god Bel's priests, Hercules, and shortly afterwards to "the devil my master" (III. 3. 141) extend far beyond Claudio's particular imagination or personality. In Borachio's speech Shakespeare invokes important issues for the audience, and he does so with a deliberation and precision that have not been sufficiently recognized.[5]

The three allusions that Borachio makes in such quick succession all call attention to their iconographic character – a reechy painting, an old church window, a worm-eaten tapestry – and they have considerable significance. The first refers to the episode in Exodus in which Moses and the Israelites passed through the Red Sea and Pharoah's soldiers were drowned. The episode was commonly understood to be a figure of baptism. The Geneva gloss of Ex. xiv, 27 reads, "So the Lord by the water saved his, and by the water drowned his enemies," and the liturgy of Baptism states the connection explicitly, praising God for leading "the children of Israel thy people through the Red Sea, figuring thereby thy holy Baptism."[6] The episode was also associated with the first commandment and in that context was related to the Redemption itself.[7] In the First Epistle to the Corinthians (x, 1–13), St. Paul touches upon all these associations and discusses both the Exodus and the meaning of baptism in terms suggesting the ideas that lie behind as well as within Borachio's speech. He asserts that the "nature of man" is lustful and open to temptations, idolatry and fornication foremost among them; that without faith in God and access to his grace, man, like Pharoah's soldiers, will be destroyed; and that the individual as well as the society of man can be saved only through the sacrament of Baptism and the profession and communion of faith it makes possible and signifies. It is significant, considering the plot that is later engineered by the Friar to redeem the marriage of Claudio and Hero, that this profession and communion, in the words of the liturgy of Baptism, "is to follow the example of our Savior Christ, and to be made like unto him, that as he died and rose again for us, so should we which are baptized die from sin, and rise again unto righteousness, continually mortifying all our evil and corrupt affections, and daily proceeding in all virtues and godliness of living."[8] As we shall see, this is essentially the process that the Friar describes in his hopes, through Hero's feigned death and rebirth, to mortify Claudio's misapprehension.

The second of Borachio's allusions, to "god Bel's priests," also focuses strongly on faithlessness and idolatry. The priests of Bel in the Apocrypha deceive the Babylonian king into believing that "an idole, called Bel" is eating and drinking the offerings that they themselves are consuming with their families in secret; but they are exposed by Daniel, who "may not worship idoles made with hands, but the living God, which hathe created the heaven & the earth, and hathe power upon all flesh."[9] The story may have come to Shakespeare's mind because, like *Much Ado*, it specifically associates the capacity to be deceived by appearances with faithlessness, but even wider connotations of idolatry are germane to the play. The medieval commonplace that the lover who is driven by lustful fantasies makes an idol of his mistress and ultimately is guilty, like Narcissus, of a pathological worship of his own image – the situation of the lover early in the *Roman de la Rose*, for example – had many Elizabethan counterparts, particularly in the sonnet sequences, and has obvious applicability to Claudio, who also, like most lovers in this tradition, has blind faith in what he himself calls the negotiation of the eye. Equally commonplace, and perhaps even more illuminating, is the Elizabethan habit of thinking of idolatry as "spiritual adultery." The metaphor is used frequently in the Scriptures and in the *Homilies*[10] and other Elizabethan commentaries. It is usually related directly both to the institution of marriage and to the second commandment, the commandment that forbids the making of "graven images" and that stresses God's jealousy.

For no man is so ignorant but that he knoweth how God in the scripture doth, by the parable of wedlock, figuratively set down the assurance and bond wherein by faith we are bound to God. God is our husband and bridegroom: we are his wife and chosen spouse. A chaste and faithful wife giveth ear alone to her husband's voice; him alone she loveth, him alone she doth obey, and, him excepted, she loveth no man at all. Again, on the other side, a shameless, faithless adulteress and whorish strumpet, not worthy to be called a wife, seemeth outwardly to stick and cleave to her husband; but privily she maketh her body common to many men, and loveth other more than her husband, and for the most part burneth on them being cold enough [toward him]. But God is a jealous God, and will be loved and worshipped alone, without any partner to rob him thereof. That is spiritual adultery and whorehunting, when men do partly love and worship God, and yet notwithstanding do therewithal give reverence to strange and other gods.[11]

The very assurance with which this sixteenth-century commentator speaks of a common understanding of "the parable of wedlock" should suggest, at the very least, that *Much Ado*'s manifest concern with adultery – in the action involving Claudio and Hero and in the very sensibilities of Benedick and Beatrice – represents something quite different from the dependence of a vulgar comedian on melodrama and obscene jests. Claudio's jealousy is the inversion of God's, and both his misconceived beliefs and Benedick's and Beatrice's fears would, for an Elizabethan, have been directly related to central tenets of the Christian understanding not only of marriage but of faith itself.[12]

Hercules, the subject of Borachio's third allusion was, of course, one of the most popular mythological figures in Renaissance art and literature. Borachio's description of him as a blatant adolescent is very unusual, but its import is clear. The heroic Hercules of the Renaissance was the Hercules at the crossroads who chose virtue instead of vice, the manly Hercules who through twelve labors rid the world of monsters. His heroic exploits were routinely interpreted in terms of the Christian psychomachia, and he himself was often regarded as a type of Christ. In *Bianthanatos* Donne linked him with Samson, "a man so exemplar, that not onely the times before him had him in Prophecy . . . and the times after him more consummately in Christ, of whom he was a Figure, but even in his own time, other nations may seem to have had some Type, or Copy of him, in *Hercules.*"[13] The figure whom Borachio describes, a "shaven" Hercules whose "cod-piece is as massy as his club," is obviously of another type altogether. Shakespeare may be thinking of Hercules' subjection to Omphale and may also be conflating that with the cutting of Samson's hair by Delilah. Both episodes were understood in the Renaissance as examples of the kind of radical unmanliness, ultimately a denial of God, that constituted Adam's submission to Eve at the Fall and that occurs in all men when their bodies and souls are not in harmony and when they worship themselves instead of God. In any event, ideas such as these seem to lie behind Borachio's portrait of a young and essentially idolatrous Hercules. I think they also inform the explicit sexual references to Hercules made elsewhere in the play both by Benedick, who fears that Beatrice "would have made Hercules have turn'd spit, yea, and have cleft his club to make the fire too" (II. 1. 222), and by Beatrice, who in her turn fears that "manhood is melted into curtsies, valour into compliment, and men are only turn'd into tongue, and trim ones too. He is now as valiant as Hercules that only tells a lie and swears it" (IV. 1. 314). It is significant, considering this context, that Don Pedro should speak of his plan to "fashion" a match between Benedick and Beatrice as "one of Hercules' labours" (II. 1. 330).

Borachio, of course, is a minor character; his homily is in any case not necessarily Shakespeare's; and, as both he and his name inform us, he is probably drunk when he makes his speech. Conrade is clearly puzzled, and the whole scene is deliberately lightened by the befuddled (though not unapt) interpolations of the listening Watch. Shakespeare, however, habitually blends the profane and the sacred, and as I suggested earlier, the apparent superfluousness of Borachio's discourse, as well as his insistence upon it in the face of Conrade's incomprehension, is a sign of its exceptional intellectual intensity. The larger envelope of Borachio's allusions, the whole subject of apparel and fashion, is one that deeply preoccupied Shakespeare, not only in this play but throughout his work. It is natural for a dramatist to be interested in the theatrical possibilities of dress for spectacle and disguise, but coordinate with that interest in Shakespeare is the pronounced Elizabethan insight, enacted in various ways in *Much Ado,* that dress and fashion can be manifestations and emblems of man's deepest sexual vanities. Parolles's spiritual bankruptcy, as we shall see, is virtually defined by the extravagance of his dress – including, not coincidentally, a massy codpiece – and so in a different way is Cloten's. In *Cymbeline,* disguises and changes of clothes have a consistent psychological and spiritual cadence. In both *All's Well* and *Cymbeline,* moreover, fashion is deeply connected with the virulence of slander and man's susceptibility to it; and in both plays the root of slander is sexual.

The seriousness with which Shakespeare treats the issue of apparel may be in part an inheritance from the medieval drama, in which Vices and devils were regularly depicted as dandies, but his conception of fashion was ultimately scriptural and was common in Elizabethan religious thought. In the sermon against excess of dress, for example, the *Homilies* warned against making "provision for the flesh, to accomplish the lusts thereof, with costly apparel"; rebuked even wives who sought to please their husbands "with the devil's attire . . . in such painted and flourished visages, which common harlots most do use"; and in a reference to 1 Pet. iii, the passage also cited in the liturgy of matrimony, advised women to "let the mind and the conscience, which is not seen with the eyes, be pure and clean; that is, saith he [Peter], an acceptable and an excellent thing before God."[14] Such an association of ideas, I think, lies behind many of the images of painted women in Shakespeare's plays,[15] including Don John's in *Much Ado,* when he slanders Hero by saying the word "disloyal" "is too good to paint out her wickedness" (III. 2. 97).

The sermon on apparel in the *Homilies* also cites St. Paul, 1 Cor. vii, 31, "where he teacheth us to use this world as though we used it not. . . ." This allusion is most significant, both because St. Paul's advice occurs in the midst of a discussion not of apparel but of marriage and because its phrasing is exceptionally suggestive. The full verse praises those "that use this worlde, as thogh they used it not: for the facion of this worlde goeth away," and it is surely this understanding of "fashion," in its larger scriptural context, that animates Borachio's digression. The whole of the seventh chapter of 1 Corinthians, as well as part of the sixth chapter, is devoted to a discussion of man's sexual impulses and of the basis and meaning of marriage. Its fundamental premise is a recognition of the combination of energy and infirmity in the flesh that clothes the human spirit. This is the profound biblical note, it seems to me, that Shakespeare strikes in the scene between Borachio and Conrade, holding us still for a few moments, as he often does in his comedies, to contemplate the deep mystery of the libidinal instincts, whose vicissitudes can either unite men in love and community or drive them into the isolation of their separate selves.

Considering this theological background, it is not surprising that Claudio and his marriage should be redeemed by an action that transparently recollects the death and resurrection of Christ, in the image of whose union with the members of the Church marriage is formed and sanctified, and whose charity is the source and the model for human love. The Friar – whose authority at the end of the play is at once gentle and sure – describes his plan for Hero's feigned death in entirely natural terms, but his speech is in obvious counterpoint to Borachio's and provides the redemptive solution to the spiritual problems that Borachio raises. The Friar speaks of changing "slander to remorse," and continues:

> But not for that dream I on this strange course,
> But on this travail look for greater birth.

He describes how often through loss

> we find
> The virtue that possession would not show us
> Whiles it was ours. So will it fare with Claudio.
> When he shall hear she died upon his words,
> Th' idea of her life shall sweetly creep

Into his study of imagination,
And every lovely organ of her life
Shall come apparell'd in more precious habit,
More moving, delicate, and full of life,
Into the eye and prospect of his soul,
Than when she liv'd indeed.

(IV. 1. 211–13, 220)

The whole weight of the play's preoccupation with fashion is brought to bear on these luminous lines, and it is difficult not to hear in them an allusion to the passage about wives in 1 Peter that is quoted in the marriage liturgy and remarked upon in the *Homilies*. Hero is clearly such a woman as the Epistle describes. Often castigated by critics for her passivity, she is quite literally mild and quiet, and her apparel is never outward even when it seems to be so. Significantly, just prior to the church scene, when Margaret makes a rather conspicuous fuss over the "rare fashion" of Hero's gown, Hero replies only, "God give me joy to wear it, for my heart is exceeding heavy" (III. 4. 13, 22–3), and it is only when her hid heart is figuratively reborn in Claudio, when she comes appareled in more precious habit into the eye and prospect of his soul, that the play approaches its comic conclusion.

CLAUDIO: Give me your hand; before this holy friar
    I am your husband, if you like of me.
HERO: And when I liv'd I was your other wife; [Unmasking.]
    And when you lov'd you were my other husband.
CLAUDIO: Another Hero!
HERO:                Nothing certainer.
    One Hero died defil'd; but I do live,
    And, surely as I live, I am a maid.
DON PEDRO: The former Hero! Hero that is dead!
LEONATO: She died, my lord, but whiles her slander liv'd.

(V. 4. 58)

As many critics have observed, Hero's rebirth is presented to Claudio as a gift of grace that he himself does little to earn. The remorse that the Friar predicts, and its accompanying psychological changes, occur only after the falsehood of the slander has been revealed, and then rather perfunctorily. It is only, as we shall see, in one of Shakespeare's last plays, in *Cymbeline*, that the process that the Friar describes is literally enacted, when Posthumus, without knowledge of Imogen's innocence, undergoes a full and explicit transformation. In *Much Ado* itself, the anatomy of transformation is plain enough in the sacrificial overtones of Claudio's and Hero's story, but the actual experience of spiritual and psychological change is displaced onto the comic relationship of Beatrice and Benedick as well as the comedy of Dogberry and the Watch, both of which drain the serious plot of its tragic potential at the same time that they absorb its deeper implications.

In most respects Benedick and Beatrice are quite different from Claudio. Both are clearly indisposed to idealize an object of love and they are both acutely conscious of precisely those sensual feelings that Claudio's romantic posture is designed to repress. It is significant that virtually the first complaint that Beatrice makes about Benedick, that he "wears his faith but as the fashion of his hat" (I. 1. 63), should be couched in language that is to have serious resonance as the play develops, and that Benedick, for his part, should refer to Beatrice as "the infernal Ate in good apparel" (II. 1. 226). Both references suggest what Benedick's and Beatrice's ceaseless scrutiny of sexual fashion in fact demonstrates, that they are burdened by the perception of man's instinctual difficulties that is expressed in Borachio's digression and that is enacted in Claudio's rejection of Hero in church. Benedick and Beatrice are hardly homilists, but the subtext of a great deal of their wit early in the play is nevertheless what the homilists of their day would have called concupiscence, and it is no accident that they should both allude, lightly but tellingly, to the legacy of Adam in describing their unwillingness to marry. Benedick proclaims, "I would not marry her though she were endowed with all that Adam had left him before he transgress'd" (II. 1. 220), and Beatrice announces that "Adam's sons are my brethren; and, truly, I hold it a sin to match in my kindred" (II. 1. 53).

Unlike Claudio, therefore, both Benedick and Beatrice "have a good eye," they "can see a church by daylight" (II. 1. 69–70), but they are not thereby spared their own erotic difficulties, and as Shakespeare shows, at the source of their inhibitions too are problems of narcissism. They both crave affection, but their very appreciation of sexuality teaches them to fear dependency, and because that fear is not only conscious but realistic, they eventually have to confront the most fundamental risk of being in love, the risk of loss through rejection or unfaithfulness. Benedick's and Beatrice's response to this possibility early in the play is an exaggerated assertion of their independence and self-sufficiency. Benedick vows to "live a bachelor" (I. 1. 212), at one point reinforcing that vow with a concatenation of the central images in the play:

> I would not marry her though she were endowed with all that Adam had left him before he transgress'd; she would have made Hercules have turn'd spit, yea, and have cleft his club to make the fire too. Come, talk not of her; you shall find her the infernal Ate in good apparel.
>
> (II. 1. 220)

All three images, as we have seen, relate Benedick's predicament directly to the preoccupations crystallized in Borachio's homily. Beatrice's protestations that it would be "a sin to match" with any of Adam's kindred are similarly connected with Borachio's imagery, and are even more explicitly sexual. In an indirect evocation of Borachio's allusion to a shaven Hercules, she claims that she "could not endure a husband with a beard on his face," but when Leonato says that she might "light on a husband that hath no beard," she answers:

> What should I do with him? Dress him in my apparel, and make him my waiting gentlewoman? He that hath a beard is more than a youth, and he that hath no beard is less than a man; and he that is more than a youth is not for me, and he that is less than a man I am not for him.
>
> (II. 1. 24)

Benedick and Beatrice, of course, protest too much, and when Don Pedro tells Benedick, after one of Benedick's declamations of independence, "I shall see thee, ere I die, look pale with love" (I. 1. 214), his expectation is also ours. The union of Benedick and Beatrice is comically inevitable. In Shakespeare's hands, however, this comic convention has more than usual power. It represents not only the obvious fact that Benedick and Beatrice's antagonism is an expression of their incipient love for one another, but also the more fundamental truth that, despite the real risks and difficulties, men and women have no choice but to love one another if they are to remain psychically and spiritually whole. In his discussion of narcissism, Freud argued that a man's libido is ultimately inseparable from his ego, that it relates to objects "much as the body of an amoeba is related to the pseudopodia which it puts out," and that this flow outwards to objects is essential, because excessive self-love, the "damming-up of libido in the ego," is not only unpleasurable but self-destructive. "A strong egoism is a protection against falling ill, but in the last resort we must begin to love in order not to fall ill, and we are bound to fall ill if, in consequence of frustration, we are unable to love."[16] Claudio's characterization is illuminated by these ideas, and the courtship of Benedick and Beatrice virtually embodies them.

That courtship, of course, culminates in Benedick and Beatrice falling in love, and Shakespeare perhaps never more profoundly explores the nature of that state than he does in the scene in which they come together after the disruption of Claudio and Hero's wedding ceremony. As I suggested earlier, Claudio's shaming of Hero, in addition to dramatizing the whole realm of human inconstancy that is invoked in Borachio's digression, specifically acts out the sexual anxieties to which Benedick and Beatrice themselves have been most subject and upon which their wit has consistently played. Beatrice, witnessing the drastic shaming of her kinswoman, has visible confirmation that

> Men were deceivers ever,
> One foot in sea and one on shore,
> To one thing constant never;
>
> (II. 3. 58)

and Benedick has the testimony of the ears and eyes of his friends, if not of his own, of the appetite and inconstancy of women. But the "proof" of their sexual anxiety paradoxically releases them from it. Benedick and Beatrice's fears of sexual instincts have a real basis, but they are also a result of repression, the same repression that spawns their wit, and as Freud suggests, when repressed, an instinct "proliferates in the dark, as it were," and seems to take on "an extraordinary and dangerous strength. . . . This deceptive strength of instinct is the result of an uninhibited development in phantasy and of the damming-up consequent on frustrated satisfaction."[17] I think that Claudio and Hero, by giving such fantasies of Beatrice and Benedick actual expression, thereby dissipate their unnatural energy. The result is that after Hero's rejection at the altar, both Beatrice and Benedick are more free to disbelieve in the evidence of what they have seen and heard and to have faith in a deeper reality of their experience.

The test of this faith for Benedick is immediate and sharp:

BENEDICK: Come, bid me do anything for thee.
BEATRICE: Kill Claudio.
BENEDICK: Ha! not for the wide world.
BEATRICE: You kill me to deny it.

(IV. 1. 286)

In the theater this celebrated exchange produces a rather uncertain combination of laughter and concern, but the very uneasiness of its tone crystallizes the serious resonance of the comic action as a whole as well as the particular complexity of this scene's spiritual and psychic movement. Literally, Benedick is asked to demonstrate that he loves Beatrice enough to believe her and fight with his best friend on her behalf. He is also asked, however, to demonstrate his superiority to the "wide world" of his senses, to kill the Claudio, figuratively the old Adam, within himself, and to invest himself totally in the object of his love. And he does so.

BENEDICK: Tarry, good Beatrice. By this hand, I love thee.
BEATRICE: Use it for my love some other way than swearing by it.
BENEDICK: Think you in your soul the Count Claudio hath wrong'd Hero?

BEATRICE: Yea, as sure as I have a thought or a soul.
BENEDICK: Enough, I am engag'd.

(IV. 1. 321)

Benedick and Beatrice are still in church and these words are in a sense a continuation of the marriage ceremony that Claudio has disrupted. They have the cadence of a betrothal, and they represent directly the kind of spiritual and psychological communion, free of inward impediment and graced by faith, that marriage is designed to celebrate. "At the height of being in love," Freud wrote in *Civilization and Its Discontents*, "the boundary between ego and object threatens to melt away. Against all the evidence of his senses, a man who is in love declares that 'I' and 'you' are one, and is prepared to behave as if it were a fact."[18] As Leonato says of Hero, in a different but related context earlier in the same scene, "Mine I lov'd . . . mine so much/That I myself was to myself not mine, /Valuing of her" (IV. 1. 136). This is the process that we see Benedick undergo in this scene, and it suggests perhaps the only, certainly the deepest, resolution of the problems of narcissism with which the whole of the play is concerned. Freud's reference to sense perceptions is particularly apposite to *Much Ado* and has wide implications in his writings, because he believed that the data of the senses stood in the same relation to external reality as those of consciousness did to the reality of the unconscious: "The unconscious is the true psychical reality; *in its inner-most nature it is as much unknown to us as the reality of the external world, and it is as incompletely presented by the data of consciousness as is the external world by the communication of our sense organs.*"[19] There is a comparable analogy in the Bible, in the famous definition of faith as "the grounde of things, which are hoped for, and the evidence of things which are not sene" (Heb. xi, 1), and both apprehensions of reality clearly animate Benedick's declaration of the faith of his love.

Benedick, and Beatrice, achieve this apprehension in part because of Claudio and Hero, who act out Benedick and Beatrice's unconscious sexual fantasies and whose ordeal literalizes the pattern of redemptive sacrifice that is the ultimate model of their faith and love, but their fundamental resource is nonetheless their own wit. And this brings me, finally, to the subject with which I began this discussion, to *Much Ado*'s extraordinary comic energy, and to Dogberry, who is the fount of this energy. It is no accident that he is the character directly responsible for discovering Don John's plot and saving Claudio and Hero. In a play in which the organs of sense are almost consistently deceived, only two groups hear and see correctly, Dogberry's and Don John's, and Dogberry and the Watch triumph largely because of their exemption from normal hearing and speech. They actually do pursue one Deformed, the vile thief of fashion who threatens to rob Claudio of the ability to love and who haunts the consciousness of Benedick and Beatrice, and they succeed in apprehending him through a power of innocence that Shakespeare comically manifests in their misuse of language. It is a power of which they themselves are certainly not conscious, though it inheres in Shakespeare's whole conception of their naiveté. "What your wisdoms could not discover," Borachio says, "these shallow fools have brought to light" (V. 1. 221). As one critic has observed, these words specifically parody 1 Cor. i, 18–19 and 27,[20] but some of the surrounding verses, especially 17, are relevant as well:

> For Christ sent me not to baptize, but to preache the Gospel, not with the wisdome of wordes, lest the crosse of Christ should be made of none effect.
> For the preaching of the crosse is to them that perish, foolishnes: but unto us, which are saved, it is the power of God.
> For it is written, I wil destroye the wisdome of the wise, and wil cast away the understanding of the prudent.
> Where is the wise? where is the Scribe? where is the disputer of this worlde? hathe not God made the wisdome of this worlde foolishnes? . . .
> But God hathe chosen the foolish things of the worlde to confounde the wise, and God hathe chosen the weake things of the worlde, to confounde the mightie things.
>
> (1 Cor. i, 17–20, 27)

These verses suggest the nature of Dogberry's great comic vitality as well as of the spiritual power of which it is the analogue. There is no clown in Shakespeare who gives us a deeper sense of joy, except perhaps Bottom, who is made to look like an ass though he is not writ down one, and who is also significantly linked to the epistle to the Corinthians.[21] We feel easily superior to Dogberry and we laugh at him, preeminently at his obvious confusion of words and sounds, but at the same time we come to understand, through that laughter, that his ignorance of the word represents a freedom that is profound and to be cherished. In a drama so concerned with the deceptions of the civilized senses and their roots in sexual anxiety, he eventually seems blessed in his childlike innocence, and our laughter at him and his watchmen brings with it a simplification of feeling and spirit not unlike that described by St. Paul.

It is interesting that malapropism should lie at the heart of the comedy that Dogberry generates. In *Jokes and Their Relation to the Unconscious*, Freud contends that the most fundamental technique of jokes is the double meaning and that its ultimate source is childhood, a period of life in which human beings are "in the habit of still treating words as things" and "tend to expect words that are the same or similar to have the same meaning behind them."[22] Freud argues that the generally uninhibited sense of play and pleasure in nonsense that is characteristic of children is surrendered only reluctantly and never completely in adult life, that the rebellion against the development of inhibitions and the sophistication of thought and feelings abides in the unconscious, and that the ultimate goal in the psychogenesis of all jokes, all comedy, and all humor, is an awakening and satisfaction of infantile pleasure. He concludes that jokes, comedy, and humor are all

agreed in representing methods of regaining from mental activity a pleasure which has in fact been lost through the development of that activity. For the euphoria which we endeavour to reach by these means is nothing other than the mood of a period of life in which we were accustomed to deal with our psychical work in general with a small expenditure of energy – the mood of our childhood, when we were ignorant of the comic, when we were incapable of jokes and when we had no need of humour to make us feel happy in our life.[23]

In the words of Sandor Ferenczi, the "one aim" of jokes and comedy and humor, is "to transport us back again for an instant to that 'Paradise Lost,' the simplicity of childhood."[24]

Dogberry, of course, is a natural inhabitant of this psychic and spiritual realm. Borachio's scriptural fool, he is also almost totally a child, expressing triumphantly, joyously, without effort or self-consciousness, the simplicity of thought and feeling that adults must work so hard to regain through laughter. He is the quintessence of the naive, which Freud considered the elemental component of comedy; he has naturally the good cheer and sense of superiority that the humorist must earn; and he continuously provides the satisfaction of jokes without intending to. He is the thing itself, and the peal of malapropisms that is his hallmark issues from the euphoric verbal play of childhood, to whose Edenic sense of absurdity, innocence, and freedom his whole characterization repeatedly returns us.

Benedick and Beatrice are seemingly at the opposite pole from him. The psychic and spiritual freedom that he has never lost, they clearly must regain. Where he is naive, they are hypersophisticated, acutely self-conscious adults, transparently inhibited, and hardly deficient in the wisdom of words. Unlike his malapropisms, their wit has complex causes and effects, it makes intellectual demands on us (and them), and the laughter it provokes is sexually tendentious and clearly intended. But Benedick and Beatrice are similar to Dogberry as well as different from him, and what becomes increasingly significant in our actual experience of the play is the recognition of their fundamental kinship. It is evident, to begin with, that they all exhibit a combination of exaggerated self-assurance and sensitivity about themselves. Benedick, proud of his wit and bachelor self-sufficiency, can easily be made uncertain of both by Beatrice:

> But that my Lady Beatrice should know me, and not know me!
> The Prince's fool! Ha! It may be I go under that title because I
> am merry. Yea, but so I am apt to do myself wrong; I am not so
> reputed; it is the base, though bitter, disposition of Beatrice

that puts the world into her person, and so gives me out. Well,
I'll be revenged as I may.

(II. 1. 180)

Beatrice, for her part, is equally vulnerable, though less obviously. She too boasts of her freedom from marriage, but she
apparently nurses an old wound from Benedick (II. 1. 246), and
there is an occasional undercurrent of apprehension in her wit:
"Good Lord, for alliance! Thus goes every one to the world but
I, and I am sunburnt; I may sit in a corner and cry 'Heigh-ho'
for a husband!" (II. 1. 286) Finally, Dogberry too can obviously
be wounded. His officiousness, which is the counterpart of
Benedick and Beatrice's wit, both reflects and protects his egotism, but it is hardly impregnable:

> Dost thou not suspect my place? Dost thou not suspect my
> years? O that he were here to write me down an ass! But,
> masters, remember that I am an ass; though it be not written
> down, yet forget not that I am an ass. No, thou villain, thou
> art full of piety, as shall be prov'd upon thee by good witness.
> I am a wise fellow; and, which is more, an officer; and, which is
> more, a householder; and, which is more, as pretty a piece of
> flesh as any is in Messina; and one that knows the law, go to;
> and a rich fellow enough, go to; and a fellow that hath had
> losses; and one that hath two gowns, and everything handsome
> about him. Bring him away. O that I had been writ down an ass!
>
> (IV. 2. 69)

The rich blend of egotism and vulnerability in this speech is the
keynote not only of Dogberry's character but of Benedick's and
Beatrice's as well.

It is not surprising, therefore, that the three of them should
appeal to our sense of pleasure in fundamentally similar ways
and that, despite the differences between Dogberry's "jokes"
and Benedick and Beatrice's, their verbal form should be essentially the same. They both depend upon a play on single words,
Dogberry's on the sound, Benedick and Beatrice's upon the
connotations, of the words. They both depend in essence upon

double meaning. This virtual identity of technique, in its turn, reveals an even deeper congruence. Freud argues that the function of the double meaning created by the kind of tendentious wit that characterizes Benedick and Beatrice "consists from the first in lifting internal inhibitions and in making sources of pleasure fertile which have been rendered inaccessible by those inhibitions."[25] He shows that the formation of double meaning in such jokes is analogous to the mechanisms of condensation and displacement in dream-work, the former a process by which a single image or word is invested with diverse meanings, many of which are not accessible to consciousness, the latter a process by which the emotion attached to one image or word is transferred to another with which it has no apparent connection in conscious thought. He argues, in addition, that the dip into these unconscious thought processes, which is the necessary constituent in the genesis of the pleasurable double meaning of such sophisticated jokes, is also the explanation of their deep affinity with their apparent opposite, the pleasurable double meanings, like Dogberry's, that are the result of naive, childish play. "For the infantile," Freud remarks,

is the source of the unconscious, and the unconscious thought-processes are none other than those – the one and only ones – produced in early childhood. The thought which, with the intention of constructing a joke, plunges into the unconscious is merely seeking there for the ancient dwelling-place of its former play with words. Thought is put back for a moment to the stage of childhood so as once more to gain possession of the childish source of pleasure.[26]

It seems to me that Freud's analysis offers a profound way of understanding the psychodynamics of Benedick and Beatrice's wit as well as its relation to the comedy of Dogberry and to the main plot. Benedick and Beatrice begin the play with a self-protective view of sexual relationships. Both of them are acutely conscious of the distance between heavenly professions and earthly instincts, between the spirit of love and the demands of its body. Their wit constitutes an assertion of this inhibiting awareness as well as an expression of its less conscious libidinal consequences, because as Hero observes of Beatrice, their wit is an instrument of self-love:

> her wit
> Values itself so highly that to her
> All matter else seems weak. She cannot love,
> Nor take no shape nor project of affection,
> She is so self-endeared.
>
> (III. 1. 52)

At the same time, however, Benedick and Beatrice's wit is a means of play and courtship, and a libidinal release. It is a defense against their unconscious impulses but also an expression that enables those impulses to work their way through fears of rejection and betrayal. The realms of affection and sensual aggressiveness that are kept separate in Claudio's consciousness are actively recognized and brought into continual juxtaposition in the process of their wit. The pleasure that they achieve in their doubles entendres – and give to us – thus begins to integrate their feelings, because in returning them to the primal source of wit it also returns them to the primal source of love itself, that period in life in which, as we have seen, pleasure is simple and direct and narcissism poses no problems, because the ego and the object are indistinguishable.

It is hardly an accident, therefore, that in that euphoric moment in which Benedick first acknowledges to himself that he is in love, the joke is palpably on him, and he comes very close to sounding like Dogberry.

> I did never think to marry. I must not seem proud; happy are they that hear their detractions and can put them to mending. They say the lady is fair; 'tis a truth, I can bear them witness; and virtuous; 'tis so, I cannot reprove it; and wise, but for loving me. By my troth, it is no addition to her wit; nor no great argument of her folly, for I will be horribly in love with her. I may chance have some odd quirks and remnants of wit broken on me because I have railed so long against marriage; but doth not the appetite alter? A man loves the meat in his youth that

he cannot endure in his age. Shall quips, and sentences, and these paper bullets of the brain, awe a man from the career of his humour? No; the world must be peopled. When I said I would die a bachelor, I did not think I should live till I were married. Here comes Beatrice. By this day, she's a fair lady; I do spy some marks of love in her.

(II. 3. 211)

Benedick has at least half his wits still about him, and these equivocations are intentional. Those that ensue after Beatrice enters are not.

BEATRICE: Against my will I am sent to bid you come in to dinner.
BENEDICK: Fair Beatrice, I thank you for your pains.
BEATRICE: I took no more pains for those thanks than you take pains to thank me; if it had been painful, I would not have come.
BENEDICK: You take pleasure, then, in the message?
BEATRICE: Yea, just so much as you may take upon a knife's point, and choke a daw withal. You have no stomach, signior; fare you well. [*Exit.*]
BENEDICK: Ha! 'Against my will I am sent to bid you come in to dinner' – there's a double meaning in that.' I took no more pains for those thanks than you took pains to thank me' – that's as much as to say 'Any pains that I take for you is as easy as thanks'. If I do not take pity of her, I am a villain; if I do not love her, I am a Jew. I will go get her picture. [*Exit.*]

(II. 3. 224)

"There's a double meaning in that" – the line is an exhilarating distillation of the play's comic experience, itself condensing sophistication and naiveté, and expressing in an instant the state of mind that is at once the goal and the source both of laughter and of love. Like Dogberry's whole characterization, it is a celebration of foolishness.

Unlike Dogberry, of course, Benedick and Beatrice are also grown-ups, and in the central part of the play, as we have seen, they are called upon to confirm the strength of their foolishness in a way that is never required of Dogberry. After the crisis is over, and Hero and Claudio are reunited, however, Beatrice and Benedick resume some of their former play of wit, though with an important difference. When what is now more purely a game threatens to revive their old inhibitions and aggressions, Benedick puts a "stop" to Beatrice's mouth by kissing her, and when Don Pedro taunts him as a "married man," he answers:

> I'll tell thee what, Prince: a college of wit-crackers cannot flout me out of my humour. Dost thou think I care for a satire or an epigram? No. If a man will be beaten with brains, 'a shall wear nothing handsome about him. In brief, since I do purpose to marry, I will think nothing to any purpose that the world can say against it; and therefore never flout at me for what I have said against it; for man is a giddy thing, and this is my conclusion.
>
> (V. 4. 99)

This is the second time that Benedick describes his being in love as a humor (Leonato associates love and humor also),[27] and though the word had a rich Renaissance heritage, its modern psychological connotations are perhaps even more to the point. In a late essay on humor, Freud cites so-called gallows humour as the paradigm of the form, as for example "When . . . a criminal who was being led out to the gallows on a Monday remarked: 'Well, the week's beginning nicely' ";[28] and it is notable that Benedick's final jest, and the last one of the whole play, is of this species: "There is no staff more reverend than one tipp'd with horn" (V. 4. 119). Freud's description of the "humourous attitude" underlying such a jest is very suggestive:

Like jokes and the comic, humour has something liberating about it; but it also has something of grandeur and elevation, which is lacking in the other two ways of obtaining pleasure from intellectual activity. The grandeur in it clearly lies in the triumph of narcissism, the victorious assertion of the ego's invulnerability. The ego refuses to be distressed by the provocations of reality, to let itself be compelled to suffer. It insists that it cannot be affected by the traumas of the external world; it shows, in fact, that such traumas are no more than occasions for it to gain pleasure.

Freud argues that the analytic explanation of this extraordinary state of mind, one that in its regressive features makes it, like love, analogous to madness, is that through the rare beneficence of the superego the humorist is "treating himself like a child and is at the same time playing the part of a superior adult towards that child."[29]

I think this formulation, with its full implications in Freudian theory, illuminates the achievement not only of Benedick and Beatrice and *Much Ado* itself, but of many other Shakespearian romantic comedies as well; for the mixture of childishness and adult indulgence that Freud discriminates in a humorous attitude is closely analogous to the simultaneous rational scepticism and irrational dilation of the spirit that constitutes Shakespeare's treatment of love in plays like *Midsummer Night's Dream* and *As You Like It*. Rosalind, like Benedick, embodies this mixture, never more clearly demonstrating her own love than when she is schooling Orlando in its follies; and the whole structure of *Midsummer Night's Dream*, in its movement from Theseus' Athens to the forest and back, serves at once as an adult comment on "what fools these mortals be" and an expressive commitment to "something of great constancy" in lovers' dreams.

In *Much Ado* a similar identification of humor and love, which Benedick makes explicit in his conclusion that man is a giddy thing and that love is a humor, is fundamental to our own experience of the play, for our response to the foolishness of the invincible ego of Dogberry is the precise counterpart of Benedick's humorous response (and ours) to the foolishness of his love. We could not enjoy Dogberry were we not ourselves adult, but at the same time the pleasure he gives us and our deep sympathy with him release us from the constraints of being grown up and allow us to recover for a moment the euphoria of the world of childhood, which is his natural home and was once ours. The same is true of Benedick's and Beatrice's feelings of love: their adult perception of sexual fashion, of the imperatives and difficulties of instinctual life, is not lost, but transformed into pleasure, redeemed by their foolish unwillingness to be beaten with brains and by their capacity to experience and enjoy a regression to that stage in childhood when the ego cannot be betrayed by its object because the two are felt as one. Both follies, theirs and Dogberry's, are associated with the spiritual childishness of faith, Dogberry's directly in the allusion to 1 Corinthians, Beatrice and Benedick's by its symbiotic relation to the whole drama of the figurative death and rebirth of Hero.

Freud himself makes an explicit analogy, in somewhat different terms, between the psychogenesis of humor and of love,[30] and he also, in another connection, makes an analogy between the state of being in love and religious faith, or at any rate, religious feeling. Freud was, of course, notoriously hostile to religion, considering it a "state of psychical infantilism" and a "mass-delusion,"[31] but he nevertheless recognized the existence of "a sensation of 'eternity,' a feeling as of something limitless, unbounded – as it were, 'oceanic,'" and he acknowledged that this transcendental feeling was a "source" of "religious energy."[32] He explained the feeling as essentially a recollection of the primary narcissism of infancy, the period upon which the deepest feelings of erotic love are also modeled:

originally the ego includes everything, later it separates off an external world from itself. Our present adult ego-feeling is, therefore, only a shrunken residue of a much more inclusive – indeed, an all-embracing – feeling which corresponded to a more intimate bond between the ego and the world about it. If we may assume that there are many people in whose mental life this primary ego-feeling has persisted to a greater or less degree, it would exist in them side by side with the narrower and more sharply demarcated ego-feeling of maturity, like a kind of counterpart to it. In that case, the ideational contents appropriate to it would be precisely those of limitlessness and of a bond with the universe.[33]

Common to the psychogenesis of all the states of mind I have described – of humor, of love, and of religious faith – is a regaining of infantile feelings whose major effect is to dilate the ego. This dilation, which corresponds exactly to St. Paul's description of the spiritual union of man and wife, if not also of man and God, is the core experience of Shakespearean comedy, explicitly sexual in the romantic comedies; more transcendental, as we shall see, in the final plays. It is the obverse of the experience of a tragedy like Othello's, in which the sense of the ego's

demarcation and isolation is intensified and in which its investment in an object of love leads to increasingly acute vulnerability, suffering, and eventually, destruction. In *Much Ado About
Nothing* the investment is protected as well as sanctioned by
Benedick's and Beatrice's humor – a humor that is ultimately an
expression of an agency of grace both within themselves and
outside of them – and the result is that the emptying of the ego
leads to its enhancement, to an intimation of the unlimited in-
clusiveness and joy it once possessed in the Eden of infancy.
The great gift of *Much Ado About Nothing* is that by a similar
process we ourselves can confirm the truth of that joy, and
experience it, in our response to Dogberry and to Benedick and
Beatrice's kinship with him.

# 4

# *Measure for Measure*

Frederick Boas, who was the first to call *Measure for Measure* and
*All's Well That Ends Well* problem plays, thought their problems
were substantive, that like Ibsen's plays they dealt with moral
issues in human life that were finally intractable. Later critics
have argued that the problems are essentially formal, that the
plays cannot successfully assimilate their own material, arous-
ing an appetite for tragedy that they do not satisfy. I think that
both complaints, and the second largely follows from the first,
stem from a modern sensibility that at once resists the plays and
overreacts to them. It judges their erotic material, especially the
bedtricks, alternately or simultaneously unseemly and superficial, and it treats their obvious theological interests as anach-
ronisms and embarrassments. Joined together these attitudes
produce an odd combination of prudery and sophistication.
The perverse drama that emerges from such a mixture was perfectly captured in the National Theatre production of *Measure
for Measure*, directed by Jonathan Miller in 1974, that concluded
with Isabella turning away in horror at the Duke's proposal of
marriage.

Even critics unsympathetic to these plays must recognize the
irresponsibility of such an interpretation, and it suggests that a
more than usual critical effort is needed not only to recover the
kind of understanding Elizabethans may have had of Shakespeare's intentions but to translate that understanding into terms
that are alive for modern spectators and readers. I think that an
attention to essentially the same psychological and spiritual inflections of love that preoccupy Shakespeare in *Othello* and

71

*Much Ado About Nothing* can be helpful, for the problem comedies are equally, and even more explicitly, concerned with the
congruence of religious and romantic faith and with the tragicomic paradoxes of erotic energy. We shall consider *Measure for Measure* in this chapter and *All's Well That Ends Well* in the next.[1]

*Measure for Measure* has an exceptionally vexing critical history. It has disturbed or antagonized critics for centuries,[2] and
almost every aspect of it is a subject of controversy in modern
criticism. It has had adherents, but the usual reaction has been
ambivalent, if not unfavorable, and the consensus of most
modern critics is that it must be judged at least a partial failure.[3]

At the root of such judgments, I think, is a fundamental unwillingness to accept *Measure for Measure's* open, and in some
respects almost clinical, inquiry into sexual appetite and aggression; but in addition and greatly complicating the criticism of it,
is a stubborn resistance to the play's equally manifest interest in
religious experience. It is astonishing how many critics are un-
willing to take the play's Christian ideas seriously.[4] Alone
among Shakespeare's plays, the very title is drawn from the
Scriptures – and not from its dark corners, but from the Sermon
on the Mount and a passage in Luke that was part of the liturgy
of the fourth Sunday after Trinity. The action is dominated by
religious images – for most of the play the Duke appears in the
habit of a friar, and Isabella appears throughout in the habit of a
novice – and the language is suffused with allusions to the Gospels, often to parables, like those of the talents and of the unmerciful servant, which were common currency. At certain
points, notably in Isabella's speech on the Atonement, both the
language and action are explicitly and deeply concerned with
the central truths of Christian experience.

To ignore such texts and images and actions, to fail particularly to consider how they might have been understood and
have affected Shakespeare's contemporary audience, would
seem a willful if not perverse procedure, and yet this is exactly
what most critics from the late seventeenth century onwards

have done. Dr. Johnson's criticism of the play is particularly instructive. He found the conclusion deeply offensive:

> The Duke has justly observed that Isabel is "importuned against all sense" to solicit for Angelo, yet here "against all sense" she solicits for him. Her argument is extraordinary.
>
> > A due sincerity govern'd his deeds,
> > 'Till he did look on me; since it is so,
> > Let him not die.
>
> That Angelo had committed all the crimes charged against him, as far as he could commit them, is evident. The only "intent" which "his act did not overtake" was the defilement of Isabel. Of this Angelo was only intentionally guilty.
>
> Angelo's crimes were such, as must sufficiently justify punishment, whether its end be to secure the innocent from wrong, or to deter guilt by example; and I believe every reader feels some indignation when he finds him spared. From what extenuation of his crime can Isabel, who yet supposes her brother dead, form any plea in his favour. "Since he was good 'till he looked on me, let him not die." I am afraid our varlet poet intended to inculcate, that women think ill of nothing that raises the credit of their beauty, and are ready, however virtuous, to pardon any act which they think incited by their own charms.[5]

Isabella's reasoning can indeed seem disconcerting, even to the play's so-called Christian critics, and we shall return to it, but what is nonetheless remarkable, aside from its sexual distaste, is how absolutely unforgiving, and specifically un-Christian, Johnson's judgment is. He insists, as so many critics have since, upon an eye for an eye, in contravention of the meaning of the scriptural sources of the play's title and of Isabella's own earlier, explicit, and eloquent plea for charity:

> Alas! alas!
> Why, all the souls that were were forfeit once;
> And He that might the vantage best have took
> Found out the remedy. How would you be
> If He, which is the top of judgment, should
> But judge you as you are? O, think on that;
> And mercy then will breathe within your lips,
> Like man new made.
>
> (II. 2. 72)

Johnson, of course, was hardly ignorant of the Bible, and as a man, hardly un-Christian, but he was always distressed by the mixture of profane and sacred material in literature, and throughout his edition of *Measure for Measure* he resolutely refuses to acknowledge biblical references, even where they are transparent. In one comment he misses an obvious allusion to the Lord's Prayer (II. 2. 158–60), and in another a reference to Paul's Epistle to the Romans (II. 2. 31–3); he castigates Warburton for a perfectly sensible reading of Lucio's lines on grace (I. 2. 24–6);[6] and he even wishes to mute the clear theological import of the speech by Isabella that I have just quoted. The lines, "And mercy then will breathe within your lips, / Like man new made," refer of course to the Redemption, as Warbuton at least partly saw when he glossed them as follows in his own edition: "The meaning is that 'mercy will add such grace to your person, that you will appear as amiable as man come fresh out of the hands of his Creator.'" But Johnson will have none of it: "I rather think the meaning is, 'you would then change the severity of your present character.' In familiar speech, 'you would be quite another man.'"[7] What readings like these demonstrate is that Johnson is in fact scandalized by the scriptural ideas of *Measure for Measure* and prefers, where he can, to remain blind to them. The realms of faith and of experience have simply become too far apart for him to reconcile.

For the generations of critics who have succeeded him, they have often become antithetical. Medieval drama has only recently escaped from the invidious assumptions that its quality increases the farther it gets from the altar, that its real vitality depends upon its comic subversion of doctrine, that its "dramatic," "human" truths are finally different from, if not incompatible with, its "religious" ideas; but these assumptions still persist in Shakespeare criticism.[8] Unfortunately, with *Measure for Measure* such prejudices are fatal, not because the dramatic experience of the play is equivalent to its theological ideas, or should be reduced to them, but because without an understanding of the play's ideas and their connotations for an Elizabethan audience, its dramatic experience is often inaccessible or unintelligible. To Shakespeare the Bible was not simply an eschatological document, but a revelation of human as well as divine truths, and to a large extent *Measure for Measure* is about the relationship between the two. Once this is appreciated, problems that have vexed scholars can be explained, if not entirely displaced, and the play can assume some coherence of thought and form. Many, if not, as the Duke says, "all difficulties are but easy when they are known" (IV. 2. 196), and the beginning of knowledge, in this case, is an apprehension of certain fundamental scriptural texts.

The most obvious are in Matthew and Luke. The passage in Matthew, which is part of the Sermon on the Mount, reads as follows:

Judge not, that ye be not judged.

For with what judgement ye judge, ye shal be judged, and with what measure ye mette, it shal be measured to you againe.

And why seest thou the mote, that is in thy brothers eye, and perceivest not the beame that is in thine owne eye?

Or how saist thou to thy brother, Suffer me to cast out the mote out of thine eye, and beholde a beame is in thine owne eye?

Hypocrite, first cast out the beame out of thine owne eye, and then shalt thou se clearely to cast out the mote out of thy brothers eye.

(Matt. vii, 1–5)

The passage in Luke is more extensive and was perhaps even better known to Elizabethans because it was part of the liturgy:

Be ye therefore merciful, as your Father also is merciful.

Judge not, and ye shal not be judged: condemne not, and ye shal not be condemned: forgive, and ye shalbe forgiven.

Give, and it shalbe given unto you: a good measure, pressed downe, shaken together and running over shal men give into your bosome: for with what measure ye mette, with the same shal men mette to you againe.

And he spake a parable unto them, Can the blinde lead the blinde? shal they not bothe fall into the ditch?

The disciple is not above his master: but whosoever *wilbe* a perfite disciple, shal be as his master.

And why seest thou a mote in thy brothers eye, and considerest not the beame, that is in thine owne eye?

Ether how canst thou saye to thy brother, Brother, let me pul out the mote that is in thine eye, when thou seest not the beame that is in thine owne eye? Hypocrite, cast out the beame out of thine owne eye first, & then shalt thou se perfectly, to pul out the mote that is in thy brothers eye.

(Luke vi, 36–42)

There is yet another and similar version in Mark iv, 21–25. All three texts were commonly associated by Elizabethan commentators with the parable of the unmerciful servant in Matt. xviii, 23–35, who, forgiven a debt of 10 thousand talents by his king, refused to forgive a debt to himself of 100 pence. Like the passage in Luke, the parable was also a regular part of the Anglican liturgy, the Gospel for the twenty-second Sunday after Trinity.

What is apparent about all these texts, even to the modern reader, is that they apply – literally chapter and verse – to the behavior of Angelo, a hypocrite who casts out a mote in his brother Claudio's eye while he has a beam in his, who will not and cannot forgive a small debt even when, after meeting Isabella, he becomes conscious of the enormity of his own. What is perhaps less apparent is the implicit stress upon the hypocritical condition of all men who do not perceive their inherent nature and the infinite mercy of Christ's Redemption. For the eventually obvious hypocrite, like Angelo, is merely a parabolic instance of the hypocritical condition of all Adam's descendants. We are all Angelos, all born with an infected will, with an immeasurable debt from which we can only be ransomed through grace.

Elizabethan commentaries on these Gospels make exactly these points, and in ways that are particularly suggestive for *Measure for Measure*. In his commentary on Luke vi, 36–42, for example, Thomas Becon writes:

For with the same measure, saith he, shall other measure to you, as you have measured with. And we can not deny but GOD hath given us good measure. For if he would have given us after our desertes, he might have plagued us with wrathe, plague, pestilence, and all evill, and put us to death, assone as we were borne. I will not rehearse how manifold waies we have offended hym, through all our life with sinnes. This might worthely be given to us as measure, even death and hell. But what doth GOD: He putteth awaie that that we have deserved, that is to saie. wrathe, indignation, judgement, death, hell, &c. and bringeth to us, heaven, grace, libertie, and a quiete mynde, from the condemnation of the lawe, and of an evill conscience ... This is truely a large and plentifull measure, but whereas thou deniest other the same measure after that, thinke not, but like measure shalbe given to thee from GOD, as thou givest other.[9]

Another commentator, Antonius Corvinus, linking the passage from Luke to the Lord's Prayer ("And forgive us our dettes, as we also forgive our detters"), remarks: "Yea if Christe wold handle us according to our wickednes which we have committed against him, and according as we have deserved, when shulde we come unto salvation?"[10] The same commentator connects the parable of the unmerciful servant in Matt. xviii with the Lord's Prayer and concludes:

The summe of this gospell is, that by grace our sins are forgiven us, wherefore we likewise ar bound, to forgive our neighbour their offences done unto us ... There is no man under heaven, but is bounde to observe the lawe, and yet nevertheless is a transgressour thereof, in especiall if god woulde contende with us in judgement ... Wherefore we must needs say, that we all are this kinges detters, that is, we be al sinners. For els how can my sinnes be forgiven me, without I felt them and knowledged them.[11]

Finally, William Perkins, in his exposition of Matt. vii, 1-5, writes:

A man must turn the eye of his mind inward, and cast his cogitations towards his owne life and conscience, that so he may see and know the principall sinnes of his owne heart and life. To this purpose serveth the morall law, which is as a glasse to let us see our maine and principall sinnes, which be the *beames* in our eyes here meant. And for direction herein I will note out some speciall maine sinnes, which be in all men naturally; and which every one must well consider of, that will cast this beame out of his owne eye.[12]

The first of the sins Perkins notes out is a "a *guiltinesse* in Adams first offence ... the sinne of mans nature," and he proceeds to the "natural disposition and proneness to every thing that is evill," which is "the second head of originall sinne"; idolatry; hypocrisy, "which naturally raigneth in all men, till grace expell it"; pride; and finally particular sin or sins.[13]

Shakespeare occasionally gave such religious sentiments explicit voice, as in Isabella's plea; in Portia's comment that "in the course of justice none of us / Should see salvation";[14] in Hamlet's remark, less expressly theological but of similar import, "use every man after his deserts, and who should scape whipping?"; and in Prospero's final words to the audience: "As you from crimes would pardon'd be, / Let your indulgence set me free." It seems to me that Shakespeare himself shared such beliefs and their implications, but in any event there is no question that in *Measure for Measure* he was interested in dramatizing them. The ultimate burden of the Gospels to which the play refers, as the commentaries universally make clear, is an apprehension, at once moral and psychological, both of the possibilities of grace in human life and of the need for it, and it is just this apprehension that the Duke wishes to make his subjects learn and Shakespeare intends for us to experience.

*Measure for Measure* begins with an ostensive emphasis upon politics and civil justice. The Duke's opening words allude to the "properties of government," and we shortly learn from his conversation with the friar that at least one of his reasons for leaving Vienna is his desire to make use of Angelo to remedy the injustices his own clemency has created:

> DUKE: We have strict statutes and most biting laws,
>        The needful bits and curbs to headstrong steeds,
>        Which for this fourteen years we have let slip;
>        Even like an o'ergrown lion in a cave,
>        That goes not out to prey. Now, as fond fathers,
>        Having bound up the threat'ning twigs of birch,
>        Only to stick it in their children's sight
>        For terror, not to use, in time the rod
>        Becomes more mock'd than fear'd; so our decrees,
>        Dead to infliction, to themselves are dead;
>        And liberty plucks justice by the nose;
>        The baby beats the nurse, and quite athwart

Goes all decorum.

FRIAR:                It rested in your Grace
To unloose this tied-up justice when you pleas'd;
And it in you more dreadful would have seem'd
Than in Lord Angelo.

DUKE:              I do fear, too dreadful.
Sith 'twas my fault to give the people scope,
'Twould be my tyranny to strike and gall them
For what I bid them do; for we bid this be done,
When evil deeds have their permissive pass
And not the punishment. Therefore, indeed, my father,
I have on Angelo impos'd the office;
Who may, in th'ambush of my name, strike home,
And yet my nature never in the fight
To do in slander.

                                   (I. 3. 19)

The immediate inspiration of these lines is almost certainly James I's discussions in *Basilicon Doron* of his own "over-deare bought experience" in "being gracious at the beginning" of his reign,[15] a fact that should alone suggest that Shakespeare did not intend them to cast doubt on the Duke's character or motives. But the intrinsic purpose of the speeches has little to do with the Duke's own character. Their function is to establish the particular situation with which he must cope and at the same time to suggest a more general moral and psychological condition.

Initially, what the Duke says anticipates the arguments Angelo employs when he himself comes to judge and even predisposes us toward them, for the Duke stresses the common Elizabethan dissociation of justice and mercy in the practice of civil law. All the homilies on Matt. vii and Luke vi, as well as the glosses in the Geneva and Genevan–Tomson Bibles, make a sharp and virtually unbridgeable distinction between the charity that must govern our souls and the justice by which we must be governed to be effective rulers, magistrates, and parents. The "indecorum" of leniency with children is the capstone of all the homiletic arguments.[16] The Duke's use of these arguments, however, is disingenuous, because he voices them eventually to disarm them. His speeches have some resemblance to the social commentary in the mystery drama – they disclose real political and social problems, but their ultimate purpose is to discriminate an unregenerate moral condition that must be redeemed rather than solved. Both the Duke's focus and the play's is not upon political or social institutions themselves, but upon the spiritual and psychological limitations and resources, the spiritual and psychological condition, of the human beings who compose them.

This focus is predominantly sexual and is immediately apparent in the subplot of *Measure for Measure*. Before the Duke even mentions the corruption of law in Vienna to the friar, we are introduced to it in the persons of Mistress Overdone, Pompey, and Lucio – a madam, a pimp, and their libertine associate, if not client. They are set strikingly before our eyes in the second scene, and the play (unlike many of its critics) never thereafter allows us to forget them. They are not merely part of its atmosphere, they constitute the very ground of its moral texture. It is through them that we learn of Claudio's predicament, it is against them that the law seems most impotent, and it is their trade of sex that we are constantly required to hold in mind as we watch the more introspective drama of sexuality played out by Angelo and Isabella. In the immediate and most important source of *Measure for Measure*, Whetstone's *Promos and Cassandra*, an underplot involving a prostitute and pimp figures very prominently in the action and is made the basis for direct homilies on man's sinful condition. Shakespeare's handling of his subplot is less explicitly homiletic and considerably richer, but its eventual effect upon us is similar. Mistress Overdone and Pompey are a projection of man's irreducible instincts, the flesh that any governor must contend with and understand, not only in his subjects, but in himself. They cannot be exorcised unless, as Pompey observes, you "geld and splay all the youth of the city" (II. 1. 218).

This is a reality of which both Angelo and Isabella are essentially ignorant and which a large measure of the Duke's plot is designed to make them experience. Significantly, at different points in the play, both of them parody the words of Paul's Epistle to the Romans (vii, 14 –15): "For we knowe that the Lawe is spiritual, but I am carnal, solde under sinne. For I alowe not that which I do: for what I wolde, that do I not: but what I hate, that do I." Isabella probably parodies the Epistle deliberately when she first tries to excuse her brother's vice, "For which I would not plead, but that I must; / For which I must not plead, but that I am / At war 'twixt will and will not" (II. 2. 31). Angelo's evocation of the verses is perhaps less conscious and occurs at the end of his unsuccessful effort to convince himself that Claudio had to be killed: "Would yet he had liv'd! / Alack, when once our grace we have forgot, / Nothing goes right; we would, and we would not" (IV. 4. 30). For both characters, however, and for Claudio as well, the Pauline words have a literal application that each of them must come to learn.

Angelo's schooling is calculated, transparent, and dramatic. The Duke deliberately tests him, leaving the city in his hands specifically to put him on trial, as he explains to the friar:

> Moe reasons for this action
> At our more leisure shall I render you.
> Only, this one: Lord Angelo is precise;
> Stands at a guard with envy; scarce confesses
> That his blood flows, or that his appetite
> Is more to bread than stone. Hence shall we see,
> If power change purpose, what our seemers be.
>
> (I. 3. 48)

As this speech, with its scriptural reference, suggests, Angelo's is a case not only of Pharisaical self-righteousness, but of severe human repression.[17] He boasts in condemning Claudio:

> When I, that censure him, do so offend,
> Let mine own judgment pattern out my death,
> And nothing come in partial.
>
> (II. 1. 29)

He does, of course, "so offend," and in a way that compels us as well as him to see his fall not simply as a particular judgment,

but as an instance of a general instinctual predicament. In her
concluding plea for her brother's life, Isabella tells him:

> Go to your bosom,
> Knock there, and ask your heart what it doth know
> That's like my brother's fault. If it confess
> A natural guiltiness such as is his,
> Let it not sound a thought upon your tongue
> Against my brother's life.

(II. 2. 136)

It is exactly at this point that Angelo, in an aside, first lets us
know of his own lust, and with a pun that is to acquire considerable significance later in the play. "She speaks, and 'tis / Such
sense that my sense breeds with it" (II. 2. 141). Shortly afterwards, when Isabella leaves, he analyzes his breeding passion in
a graphic and psychologically penetrating soliloquy:

> What's this, what's this? Is this her fault or mine?
> The tempter or the tempted, who sins most?
> Ha!
> Not she; nor doth she tempt; but it is I
> That, lying by the violet in the sun,
> Do as the carrion does, not as the flow'r,
> Corrupt with virtuous season. Can it be
> That modesty may more betray our sense
> Than woman's lightness? Having waste ground enough,
> Shall we desire to raze the sanctuary,
> And pitch our evils there? O, fie, fie, fie!
> What dost thou, or what are thou, Angelo?
> Dost thou desire her foully for those things
> That make her good? O, let her brother live!
> Thieves for their robbery have authority
> When judges steal themselves. What, do I love her,
> That I desire to hear her speak again,
> And feast upon her eyes? What is't I dream on?
> O cunning enemy, that, to catch a saint,
> With saints dost bait thy hook! Most dangerous
> Is that temptation that doth goad us on
> To sin in loving virtue. Never could the strumpet,
> With all her double vigour, art and nature,
> Once stir my temper; but this virtuous maid

Subdues me quite. Ever till now,
When men were fond, I smil'd and wond'red how.

(II. 2. 162)

This speech is an anatomy of repression. Long dammed up, Angelo's sexual sense is now emerging violently, but in a way still calculated to humiliate both its object and himself. Angelo perceives some of the reason for this "corruption" in his comparison of the rotting carrion and the blossoming flower. He is less aware that he is attracted to his mirror-image in Isabella and that the act with her he dreams on is therefore necessarily burdened with the destructive ambivalence of his feelings about his own exalted purity. The whole of the speech is an exploration of the violence that a man can inflict upon himself (and others) when he attempts to deny the reality of his body, a condition that in both scriptural and Freudian thought rests upon an unrelieved sense of guilt.

Through the Duke's plot, Angelo eventually comes to terms with his guilt, and the spiritual process of his understanding, though not elaborated in detail, is explicit and clear. After his soliloquy, he solicits Isabella – "Nay, but hear me; / Your sense pursues not mine" (II. 4. 73) – and condemns her brother without mercy; and though he can recognize that his blood is mustering to his heart, "Making both it unable for itself / And dispossessing all my other parts / of necessary fitness" (II. 4. 21), he remains entirely its creature until the moment when he stands totally exposed before the Duke and his community. Then he changes, and once again swiftly. For the first time his awareness of his condition becomes partially redeeming:

O my dread lord,
I should be guiltier than my guiltiness,
To think I can be undiscernible,
When I perceive your Grace, like pow'r divine,
Hath look'd upon my passes. Then, good Prince,
No longer session hold upon my shame,
But let my trial be mine own confession:
Immediate sentence then, and sequent death,
Is all the grace I beg.

(V. 1. 364)

His next speech, spoken after Isabella pleads for his life and before Claudio is revealed alive, is that of a genuinely penitent man. Escalus laments that he should have slipped "so grossly, both in the heat of blood / And lack of temper'd judgment afterward," and Angelo answers:

> I am sorry that such sorrow I procure;
> And so deep sticks it in my penitent heart
> That I crave death more willingly than mercy;
> 'Tis my deserving, and I do entreat it.

(V. 1. 470)

These brief words, and the state of thought and feeling they reveal, are convincing not only because they are theologically to the point, but also because they are informed by what we know to be Angelo's considerably enlarged experience of his own sexual nature. Angelo's greatest crime, the one for which Johnson fails to indict him, and the only one that the play allows to have real effect, is against himself, and his whole experience with Isabella and Mariana is at once a punishment for this crime and an expiation of it. As the Duke intends, he is brought to confess that his blood flows, and this "confession" is a psychic as well as spiritual release. One of Freud's comments on the process of psychoanalysis has particular relevance to the Duke's treatment of Angelo:

To believe that psycho-analysis seeks a cure for neurotic disorders by giving a free rein to sexuality is a serious misunderstanding which can only be excused by ignorance. The making conscious of repressed sexual desires in analysis makes it possible, on the contrary, to obtain a mastery over them which the previous repression had been unable to achieve. It can more truly be said that analysis sets the neurotic free from the chains of his sexuality. [18]

It seems to me that this process corresponds closely to the Duke's method and purpose in testing Angelo. As in *All's Well*, the bedtrick itself, with its controlled combination of the actuality as well as the fantasy of sexual aggression, is critical, but Angelo's increasing consciousness of the desires within himself is an equally important part of the process that frees him from their tyranny and from the consequent burden of his censorious

judgment. This continous process of release through recognition, which both he and we experience, authenticates his libera-
tion from hypocrisy and allows us to accept the promise of his
marriage at the end of the play.

Isabella is subjected to a similar process, though the beam in
her eye is smaller than Angelo's and its perception, both by her
and by us, more subtle. She is certainly fully devoted to the
religious ideas she argues before Angelo, but her idealism, not
unlike his, is inexperienced and based on an ignorance of her
own human composition. It is significant that she is first introduced to us immediately following the Duke's speech declaring
that Angelo "scarce confesses / That his blood flows" (there
would be a virtual montage of this speech and her appearance
on an Elizabethan stage), and that she is shown not only about
to enter a nunnery, but "wishing a more strict restraint" in its
rules. Because those rules are already conspicuously severe –
"you must not speak with men / But in the presence of the
prioress; / Then, if you speak, you must not show your face, /
Or, if you show your face, you must not speak" (I. 4. 4, 10–13) –
the character of her zeal arouses our interest from the start.
Moreover, her habit and prospective profession are themselves
probably intended to evoke the kind of response, equivocal at
best, that Shakespeare makes explicit in *A Midsummer Night's
Dream* when Theseus warns Hermia that if she disobeys her
father she must either die or

> endure the livery of a nun,
> For aye to be in shady cloister mew'd
> To live a barren sister all your life,
> Chanting faint hymns to the cold fruitless moon.
> Thrice-blessed they that master so their blood
> To undergo such maiden pilgrimage;
> But earthlier happy is the rose distill'd
> Than that which withering on the virgin thorn
> Grows, lives, and dies, in single blessedness.
>
> (I. 1. 70)

Theseus' thought is a modulation of the parable of the talents,
and, as we shall see, there is an emphasis upon that parable in

*Measure for Measure* that makes his speech particularly apposite to Isabella.

Isabella's debates with Angelo are in themselves probably meant to be problematic. An Elizabethan audience would hardly have regarded chastity as a technicality, and Angelo's assault, in addition, amounts to a rape. On the other hand, there is truth to the assertion, even though Angelo makes it, that "our compell'd sins / Stand more for number than for accompt" (II. 4. 57), and there is, as Angelo also points out, a cruelty fully equal to the law's in her refusal to save her brother's life. Shakespeare seems deliberately to have complicated his sources to make their debate as equivocal as possible. What is not equivocal, however, is Isabella's subsequent behavior with Claudio. When she visits him in prison and explains Angelo's proposal, he wavers and cries out to her:

> Sweet sister, let me live.
> What sin you do to save a brother's life,
> Nature dispenses with the deed so far
> That it becomes a virtue.
>
> (III. 1. 134)

An argument not entirely unlike Angelo's, but this time from her brother, who is on the verge of death and afraid, and to this appeal her only response is bewilderment and panic. Her hysteria in fact shows how deeply moved she is by his feelings and fear, but she nonetheless has little room for compassion. She has argued eloquently from Christ's example of the need for mercy, but at this moment of trial and threat, in her own heart, for her own brother, she can find none:

> O you beast!
> O faithless coward! O dishonest wretch!
> Wilt thou be made a man out of my vice?
> Is't not a kind of incest to take life
> From thine own sister's shame? What should I think?
> Heaven shield my mother play'd my father fair!
> For such a warped slip of wilderness
> Ne'er issu'd from his blood. Take my defiance;
> Die; perish. Might but my bending down

Reprieve thee from thy fate, it should proceed.
I'll pray a thousand prayers for thy death,
No word to save thee.

(III. 1. 137)

There can be extenuation, but no excuse for such words. Just as surely as Angelo, Isabella betrays the ideals by which she wishes to live, and she does so, like Angelo, because she cannot accept the reality of human instincts. As a number of critics have noticed, there is a strong erotic undercurrent in her characterization. Angelo's lust for her at first seems entirely a permutation of his own psyche, but I think we are eventually meant to understand that she herself also offers unconscious sexual provocation. There is a hint in Claudio's description of why she might succeed with Angelo:

for in her youth
There is a prone and speechless dialect
Such as move men; beside, she hath prosperous art
When she will play with reason and discourse,
And well she can persuade.

(I. 2. 175)

But if the equivocation of "prone," "move," and "play" are only suggestive (and seem like overreadings), the erotic drift of at least one of her own speeches is unmistakable. When Angelo asks her, hypothetically, if she would not sacrifice her virginity to save Claudio, she answers:

As much for my poor brother as myself;
That is, were I under the terms of death,
Th' impression of keen whips I'd wear as rubies,
And strip myself to death as to a bed
That longing have been sick for, ere I'd yield
My body up to shame.

(II. 4. 99)

This intense speech is not called for by the argument; it is an internal eruption. Aside from the obvious suggestion of masochism, what it conveys, and Isabella's subsequent abuse of her brother (including the hysterical image of incest) confirms, is that she is afraid not only of Angelo's desires, but of her own.

It is in this context that her behavior in the final acts of the play must be understood. After witnessing the scene between her and Claudio in prison, the Duke praises her: "The hand that hath made you fair hath made you good" (III. 1. 179); but he proceeds at the same time to place her in a situation that will expand her understanding both of herself and others. He keeps her ignorant of the fact that Claudio is alive; he stages an elaborate role for her that, however fictive, nonetheless compels her to appear at length before the whole community and publicly shame herself; and perhaps most important, he involves her intimately with the arrangements for the bedtrick and with Mariana, a woman whose sexual desires are at once open and legitimate. Nothing is clearer in a stage production than that Mariana wants her man, and far from being a scandal, it is an education for Isabella to help her get him. For when at the end of the play Mariana kneels to ask her to plead for Angelo, and when the Duke, invoking the ghost of Claudio, says "Against all sense you do importune her," it is precisely with a dilated understanding of sense that she is able to respond. She kneels to the Duke, and says:

> Most bounteous sir,
> Look, if it please you, on this man condemn'd,
> As if my brother liv'd. I partly think
> A due sincerity govern'd his deeds
> Till he did look on me; since it is so,
> Let him not die. My brother had but justice,
> In that he did the thing for which he died;
> For Angelo,
> His act did not o'ertake his bad intent,
> And must be buried but as an intent
> That perish'd by the way. Thoughts are no subjects;
> Intents but merely thoughts.
>
> (V. 1. 441)

That Isabella should thus argue her case in terms of law, not Christ, and particularly that she should refer to her own effect upon Angelo, is not a betrayal of religious faith, but an exemplification of it. However legally tenuous it may be, her plea – in behalf of the man who she thinks executed her brother – is surely an extraordinary enactment of the kind of mercy for which she had argued in theory before; and it is made possible precisely because her recognition of her own femininity has taught her the human need for mercy. Her sexual awareness is not vanity, but humility.

The deepest education in humility, however, is reserved for Claudio, the third of the characters of whom the Duke makes trial, and with Claudio the recognition of the nature of human instincts is extended beyond sexuality to the whole Pauline realm of the flesh, including mortality itself. His predicament is from the first represented with deeply paradoxical overtones. On the one hand, placed at the opposite pole from the repressed behavior of Isabella and Angelo, his fertile intercourse with the woman to whom he is betrothed and whom he loves seems both natural and life-giving, and most of the characters in the play regard Angelo's judgment upon him with a mixture of bemusement and pain. After failing to change Angelo's mind, Escalus worries more about Angelo's weakness than Claudio's: "Well, heaven forgive him! and forgive us all! / Some rise by sin, and some by virtue fall" (II. 1. 37); and the "gentle Provost" twice expresses a sympathy for Claudio that we ourselves are clearly expected to share:

> Alas,
> He hath but as offended in a dream!
> All sects, all ages, smack of this vice; and he
> To die for't!
>
> (II. 2. 3)

The Provost's second comment, made directly to the disguised Duke, is even more indignant:

> She is with child;
> And he that got it, sentenc'd – a young man
> More fit to do another such offence
> Than to die for this.
>
> (II. 3. 12)

On the other hand, directly after this speech the Duke solemnly shrives Juliet, and neither she nor Claudio ever treat what they have done lightly. On the contrary, from the very beginning, when he is first apprehended, Claudio speaks of his sexual relations with Juliet with marked ambivalence. He protests against Angelo's tyrannical use of authority and against the excessiveness of his punishment, but at the same time, when Lucio jestingly asks him, "Whence comes this restraint?" his answer is astringent and disquieting:

> From too much liberty, my Lucio, liberty;
> As surfeit is the father of much fast,
> So every scope by the immoderate use
> Turns to restraint. Our natures do pursue,
> Like rats that ravin down their proper bane,
> A thirsty evil; and when we drink we die.
>
> (I. 2. 118)

Shakespeare is habitually interested in the ways in which opposites merge (the lines of Escalus just quoted are an example), and in this play in particular, in which he deals so extensively with sexual repression, an interest in sexual license is almost a dialectical necessity. Claudio's speech is related to the conception of unrestrained appetite explored in *Troilus and Cressida*, "an universal wolf" and "an universal prey" that ends by eating itself (I. 3. 121); and there is perhaps as well an undercurrent of the familiar Renaissance pun on "die," equating death with sexual consummation.

Dialectical symmetry alone, however, cannot account for the starkness of Claudio's imagery nor for the sense that Shakespeare extends Claudio's whole predicament beyond the bounds of the sexual instinct alone. Claudio's speech describes a process, not simply a moment of pleasure; he himself continuously faces the prospect of death as a direct result of his sexual actions; and the Duke, who prolongs that confrontation, also pointedly generalizes upon its significance, suggesting that the sensual impulses that have animated Claudio are themselves modulations of the deeper reality of his movement towards

death. In his disguise as a friar, the Duke counsels Claudio to
"Be absolute for death; either death or life / Shall thereby be the
sweeter," and he rehearses for him a litany of man's frailties: "A
breath thou art ... thou art Death's fool; / For him thou labour'st
by thy flight to shun / And yet run'st toward him still. Thou art
not noble ... Thou'rt by no means valiant ... Thy best of rest is
sleep, / And that thou oft provok'st; yet grossly fear'st / Thy
death, which is no more. Thou art not thyself ... Happy thou
art not ... Thou art not certain ... If thou art rich, thou'rt
poor ... Friend hast thou none"; and he concludes:

> Thou hast nor youth nor age,
> But, as it were, an after-dinner's sleep,
> Dreaming on both; for all thy blessed youth
> Becomes as aged, and doth beg the alms
> Of palsied eld; and when thou art old and rich,
> Thou hast neither heat, affection, limb, nor beauty,
> To make thy riches pleasant. What's yet in this
> That bears the name of life? Yet in this life
> Lie hid moe thousand deaths; yet death we fear,
> That makes these odds all even.
>
> (III. 1. 5)

There is not a word in this well-known speech of Christ or
salvation, but there does not need to be. The friar is the Duke,
and I think we are confident, even at this point in the action,
that he has no intention of administering the last sacrament
because he has no intention of letting Claudio die. His fundamental purpose, moreover, in this speech as in the entire action
of the play, is not to set down what is in heaven, but the reality
of man's condition on earth that inspires belief in heaven. The
attitudes he expresses – which are distilled from a reservoir of
classical as well as medieval and Renaissance thought on death –
were the conventional premises of Christian faith. In an essay
entitled, "That to Philosophie, is to learne how to die," upon
which Shakespeare may well have drawn in the Duke's speech,
Montaigne observes that "Our religion hath had no surer
humane foundation, than the contempt of life."[19] It is this
human foundation that the Duke intends, and unlike many crit-

ics of the play, Claudio at least does not misunderstand him. He
says to the Duke:

> I humbly thank you.
> To sue to live, I find I seek to die;
> And, seeking death, find life. Let it come on.
>
> (III. 1. 41)

In the Gospel according to St. Matthew (xvi, 25), these lines
read: "For whosoever wil save his life, shal lose it: and
whosoever shal lose his life for my sake, shal finde it." That
Claudio should subsequently falter and desperately cling for a
moment to life is not an argument against this faith but a proof
of its truth and its urgency.

Another, and crucial, point to be made, not only about the
Duke's speech and Claudio's answer to it, but about the whole
configuration of Claudio's experience in the play, is that a
proper appreciation of the reality of death is redemptive in
purely human terms as well, because it leads finally not to a
denial of life, but to a deeper understanding and enrichment of
it, literally to its inspiration. This is the paradox that clearly
interested Montaigne, and it has at least a partial counterpart,
very relevant to this play, in Freud. The emphasis of Freud's
psychoanalytic theory is clearly on the sexual instinct, in its
largest sense Eros, which is governed by the pleasure principle
and which gives and protects life; but his practice and thinking
increasingly compelled him to deal with forces in human existence that were either analogues of death (preeminently sadism
and masochism) or that seemed to lead to it, and in *Beyond the
Pleasure Principle* he posited a death instinct. Professedly meta-
psychological and speculative, the essay is not altogether coherent or persuasive, but certain of its leading ideas are clear and
helpful in understanding *Measure for Measure*. Arguing from the
premise based on much of his previous work, *"that an instinct is
an urge inherent in organic life to restore an earlier state of things,"*
Freud remarks that:

If we are to take it as a truth that knows no exception that everything
living dies for *internal* reasons – becomes inorganic once again – then

we shall be compelled to say that '*the aim of all life is death*' and, looking backwards, that '*inanimate things existed before living ones*'.[20]

Freud acknowledges that our instincts of self-preservation would seem to contradict such an aim, but he concludes, reluctantly, that seen in the light of the evidence of a death instinct,

the theoretical importance of the instincts of self-preservation, of self-assertion and of mastery greatly diminishes. They are component instincts whose function it is to assure that the organism shall follow its own path to death, and to ward off any possible ways of returning to inorganic existence other than those which are immanent in the organism itself. We have no longer to reckon with the organism's puzzling determination (so hard to fit into any context) to maintain its own existence in the face of every obstacle. What we are left with is the fact that the organism wishes to die only in its own fashion.[21]

Barnardine, who is "insensible of mortality and desperately mortal" (IV. 2. 137), and whose virtually comatose insistence upon life is so potent in performances of *Measure for Measure*, is a direct animation of the paradox Freud describes. In the remainder of the essay, Freud insists on the dualism of the paradox, firmly distinguishing "two kinds of instincts: those which seek to lead what is living to death, and others, the sexual instincts, which are perpetually attempting and achieving a renewal of life." At the same time he feels compelled to "suppose" death instincts "to be associated from the very first with life instincts," and he concludes that "the pleasure principle seems actually to serve the death instincts."[22] The whole of *Beyond the Pleasure Principle* illuminates the treatment of death in *Measure for Measure* and particularly the peculiar synapse of thought, found in *All's Well That Ends Well* too, by which Shakespeare so closely and intricately associates the immanence of death not only with the perversion of sexual energy but with its natural expression.

Montaigne exhibits an essentially similar conception of death in the essay I have already cited. In a passage that is largely a paraphrase of Seneca and Lucretius, he writes:

It is the condition of your creation: death is a part of your selves: you flie from your selves. The being you enjoy, is equally shared betweene life and death. The first day of your birth doth as wel addresse you to die, as to live. . . .

All the time you live, you steale it from death: it is at her charge. The continuall worke of your life, is to contrive death; you are in death, during the time you continue in life: for, you are after death, when you are no longer living. Or if you had rather have it so, you are dead after life: but during life, you are still dying: and death doth more rudely touch the dying, than the dead, and more lively and essentially. If you have profited by life, you have also beene fed thereby, depart then satisfied. [23]

The word "profit," however, introduces a distinctly medieval and Renaissance inflection to the idea of death, which is at most only implicit in Freud, but very important in Shakespeare. Montaigne argues not only that death is the inner purpose of life, but that the active recognition of that purpose should inform the way we live. "Life in it selfe," he remarks, "is neither good nor evill: it is the place of good or evill, according as you prepare it for them. . . . Wheresoever your life endeth, there is it all. The profit of life consists not in the space, but rather in the use."[24]

This turn of thought is habitual in both Montaigne and Shakespeare, and their common source is the parable of the talents in Matt. xxv, 14–30, and Luke xix, 12–27, scriptural texts that have particularly deep resonance in *Measure for Measure* (and also, as we shall see, in *All's Well That Ends Well*), informing the Duke's trial not only of Claudio, but of all the characters in the play. The parable describes a lord, about to depart on a long journey, who summons his servants to him:

And unto one he gave five talents, and to another two, & to another one, to everie man after his own habilitie, & straight way went home.

Then he that had received the five talents, went and occupied with them, and gained other five talents.

Likewise also, he that *received* two, he also gained other two.

But he that received that one, went & digged it in ye earth, & hid his masters money.

(Matt. xxv, 15–18)

When the lord returns he praises the faithfulness of the first two
servants, but condemns the wickedness of the last:

> Thou evil servant, & slothful, thou knewest that I reap where I sowed
> not, and gather where I strawed not.
> Thou oghtest therefore to have put my money to the exchangers, and
> then at my comming shulde I have received mine owne with vantage.
>
> (Matt. xxv, 26–7)

The parable had a rich exegetical history in the Middle Ages,[25]
but its essential force remained undiminished in the Elizabethan
period as well: that we must make a spiritual investment and a
spiritual profit of our own lives. As the Geneva gloss (1560) put
it: "This similitude teacheth how we oght to continue in the
knowledge of God, and do good with those graces yt God hathe
given us."

The parable clearly preoccupied Shakespeare in the sonnets
and elsewhere, and he may have been specifically led to it in
*Measure for Measure* by a process of association with the talents
mentioned in the parable of the unmerciful servant in Matt.
xviii. In any event, like the lord in the parable of the talents, the
Duke leaves on an indefinite journey, summoning his servants
and committing his powers to them. His departing speech is
particularly suggestive. Before Angelo appears he asks Escalus,
"What figure of us think you he will bear?" and to Angelo himself he says:

> Angelo,
> There is a kind of character in thy life
> That to th' observer doth thy history
> Fully unfold. Thyself and thy belongings
> Are not thine own so proper as to waste
> Thyself upon thy virtues, they on thee.
> Heaven doth with us as we with torches do,
> Not light them for themselves; for if our virtues
> Did not go forth of us, 'twere all alike
> As if we had them not. Spirits are not finely touched
> But to fine issues; nor Nature never lends
> The smallest scruple of her excellence

> But, like a thrifty goddess, she determines
> Herself the glory of a creditor,
> Both thanks and use.
>
> (I. 1. 27)

This speech is a clear injunction to Angelo to use his credit with vantage, and the financial imagery, with its traditional spiritual connotations, is unmistakable and insistent.[26] Angelo intensifies its import by picking up and playing upon the figure of coining:

> Now, good my lord,
> Let there be some more test made of my metal,
> Before so noble and so great a figure
> Be stamp'd upon it.
>
> (I. 1. 48)

The play upon the word "metal," whose spelling was at that time interchangeable with "mettle," is almost an exact analogue of the metaphorical extension of the word "talent" in the parable.

Images of investment and coining persist in the remainder of the play and are turned, with remarkable literalness, to the central issue of the action: human coinage and usury, sexual intercourse and procreation. "It were as good," Angelo lectures Isabella at the start of their second interview,

> To pardon him that hath from nature stol'n
> A man already made, as to remit
> Their saucy sweetness that do coin heaven's image
> In stamps that are forbid; 'tis all as easy
> Falsely to take away a life true made
> As to put metal in restrained means
> To make a false one.
>
> (II. 4. 42)

Moments later, he asks her if she would not, if necessary, procure "credit" with her brother's judge by laying down "the treasures" of her body, and she replies that to yield to such shame would be ignominious "ransom," that her brother's death would be "the cheaper way," and that she does something "excuse the thing I hate / For his advantage that I dearly love" (II. 4.

92, 96, 111, 105, 119-20). Angelo then remarks, "We are all
frail... Nay, women are frail too," and Isabella rejoins:

> Ay, as the glasses where they view themselves,
> Which are as easy broke as they make forms.
> Women, help heaven! Men their creation mar
> In profiting by them. Nay, call us ten times frail;
> For we are soft as our complexions are,
> And credulous to false prints.
>
> (II. 4. 121, 124, 125-30)

The same sentiment and imagery are echoed in the subplot afterwards, when Elbow castigates Pompey for his trade:

ELBOW: Nay, if there be no remedy for it, but that you will needs buy
    and sell men and women like beasts, we shall have all the
    world drink brown and white bastard.
DUKE: O heavens! what stuff is here?
POMPEY: 'Twas never merry world since, of two usuries, the merriest
    was put down, and the worser allow'd by order of law a
    furr'd gown to keep him warm; and furr'd with fox on lamb-
    skins too, to signify that craft, being richer than innocency,
    stands for the facing.

> (III. 2. 1)

The deep relation between the two usuries is expressed in the
two senses of "angel" in Angelo's very name, as the Duke
suggests when he laments for him:

> O, what may man within him hide,
> Though angel on the outward side!
>
> (III. 2. 253)

The scriptural implications of these images of coining and
profit sustain themselves, but they are in addition deepened by
their frequent collocation with another train of images elicited
(again with conspicuous literalness) by the play's title and primary scriptural source: images of measuring, weighing, scaling,
grading, and testing. Angelo, at the very start, questions the
Duke's "test" both of his "metal" and "mettle." At the end of

their second meeting, after Isabella protests that she will denounce him, Angelo asserts, "Say what you can: my false o'erweighs your true" (II. 4. 170); Claudio wishes his sister to "assay" Angelo (I. 2. 174); Lucio bids her to "assay the power" she has (I. 4. 76); and the Duke tells Claudio that Angelo's proposal to her had been designed only to make "an assay of her virtue" (III. 1. 160). Then, as now, the word "assay" meant both to measure the nature and quality of a person or the composition and purity of a metal.

The cumulative result of these configurations of images and actions in *Measure for Measure* is to compel us to understand man's instincts, and particularly sexuality, as a form of spiritual and psychic capital that must be invested to realize the deeper purposes of human life, purposes that ultimately include death itself. The Duke makes his subjects realize that the state of Vienna is within themselves, a moral and psychological condition, a beam in their own eyes. In the words of the homilist, which could also be Freud's, he makes them turn the eyes of their minds inwards so that they may recognize the mortal conditions of their own lives and hearts. He also, however, and this is the ultimate purpose of his deceptions and contrivances, enables them to find a redeeming and fruitful expression of their humanity by bringing them to marriage. Though not a sacrament in the Anglican liturgy, marriage always in Shakespeare has sacramental value, and never more than in *Measure for Measure*, where it is seen as the deepest and most creative model and expression of human community, as the means through procreation by which we can make true coin of the currency of our lives, by which we can – literally – remake ourselves in the image of our Creator. It is thus the most perverse combination of Victorian prudery and modern cynicism to regard the bedtrick as simply an archaic convention or to imagine that Isabella should recoil from the Duke's proposal at the end of the play. The bedtrick miraculously transforms Angelo's destructive libidinousness, liberating his manhood and turning it to the consummation of a betrothal he had betrayed, and the Duke's proposal offers the promise that in marriage Isabella can fully express her newborn awareness of herself as a woman. The one action moderates scope, the other restraint – the two poles of sexuality in the play – and both are at once gracious and life-giving.

Objections to the bedtrick and Isabella's marriage with the Duke are only symptoms, of course, of a larger category of modern discomfort with *Measure for Measure*, the dissatisfaction with its form. There are various, though related, arguments against the form of the play: that the Duke is incoherent as a character, a manipulative deus ex machina represented in incompatible naturalistic and allegorical modes; that Shakespeare depicts Claudio, if not Isabella, in essentially ambivalent ways; and above all, that the play arouses an expectation of tragedy that it cannot fulfill and indeed willfully denies. "The first half of the play shows us what is in fact the case; the second half is escapist fiction."[27] Though ostensibly formal, such objections rest to a considerable extent upon a fundamental misapprehension of the play's ideas. As I have tried to make clear, the grace offered and achieved at the end of *Measure for Measure*, rather than contradicting the spiritual and psychic experiences of the beginning, is their consequence and is inherent within them. It is an understanding of "what is in fact the case" about human behavior that makes possible its most charitable expression in forgiveness and creativity; and the Duke, in bringing his subjects to such an understanding, combines his spiritual, psychological, and political roles by reconstituting both their souls and the soul of his society. Elizabethans would have appreciated, even if we do not, that

All temtation or tryal is not evell. For God tempteth his servantes: one freend is tempted of another: the childe is tryed by the Father, the Wyfe by her Husbande. the Servaunt by his Master, not that they might be hurt by triall, but rather that they might thereby be profited.[28]

So, surely, are the characters who are tempted and tried in *Measure for Measure*, and if the full theological basis for this conception of profit is now lost to us, we can still recognize, in terms that remain close to those of the parable, that an untried self is a buried self.

If, however, the failure to understand these ideas is the final cause of critical anxiety about the play's form, the efficient cause, and one that is endemic in Shakespeare criticism, is the failure to appreciate its dramaturgy, the way it is designed to affect an audience, on stage, in performance; and it is with this subject that we must finally deal. To begin with, one would hardly guess in reading the pages of many of its critics that the play is often funny. The most insistent comedy, of course, occurs in the subplot, which is as important to the tonal texture of the play as to its intellectual substance. Before the main action develops, we are introduced to a judgment scene (II. 1), the play's first, which is dominated by a mélange of Elbow's malapropisms and Pompey's puns, and a similar mood, broad and usually bawdy, is sustained whenever the low-life characters appear. The prison itself, a central image as well as location of the play's action, is transformed by them. Pompey remains as "well acquainted" – and as witty – there as he was in his own "house of profession" (IV. 3. 1–2), and even Master Barnardine, as I've mentioned, "unfit to live or die" (IV. 3. 60), stays undaunted and resolutely comic.

Equally resolute, and even more insistent on stage than the subplot, is the complex comedy of Lucio. His role is particularly apparent in performance, where his ubiquitousness is matched only by the Duke's. He pops up everywhere, moving freely through both plots, acting pervasively as a sardonic commentator. He has jokes for everyone and for all occasions – for Claudio, for Isabella, for Pompey, and for the Duke, especially for the Duke. Early in the play he shows some affection for Claudio and possibly admiration for Isabella, to whom he delivers a speech that explicitly and richly describes the fruitfulness of human generation (I. 4. 40–4), but as the play proceeds, his libertine wit becomes progressively more sterile and irreverent until finally, with the Duke, it ends in outright slander. For us, given the theatrical situation, the slanders are comic, but the

Duke himself is conspicuously not amused. His irritation is itself funny, but it should not be construed, as it has been by many modern critics, as vindictive or petty; for Lucio, who becomes the Duke's comic shadow, is also his most serious antagonist. His slanderousness, for Elizabethans, would have marked him as a kin of the Blatant Beast, an enemy both of social and moral order, and would have related him quite directly to the underlying religious ideas of the play. William Perkins considered slander to be the essential subject of Matt. vii, 1–5. The verse, "Judge not, that ye be not judged," he read as a reference to "rash judgment" and as specifically an injunction against slanderers:

He that gives rash judgment of another, is worse then a theefe that steales away a mans goods: for he robbes him of his *good name*, which (as Saloman saith) *is to be chosen above great riches*, Prov. 22. 1. Againe, riches may be restored, so can not a mans good name beeing once blemished in the hearts of many. Againe, a man may defend himselfe from a theefe, but no man can shunne an other mans evill minde, or his badde tongue: nay, the backbiter is worse then a murtherer, for he killeth three at once; first, his *owne soule* in thus sinning: secondly, his *neighbour* whose name he hurteth: and thirdly, the hearer who receiveth this rash and injust report: and for this cause the *slaunderer* is numbered among those that shall not inherit the kingdome of God, Psal. 15. 3, 1 Cor. 6. 10, and the Apostle chargeth Christians to account such raylers as of persons excommunicate, 1 Cor. 5. 11.[29]

Lucio is such a soul as Perkins describes. His licentiousness has the excuse neither of trade, like Pompey's, nor passion, like Angelo's, and his condition is even more desperate than the drunken Barnardine's, because it is so consciously faithless. Believing neither in the reality of death nor the talents of life, he ultimately reduces all people and actions, all human relationships, to the sexual "game of tick-tack" (I. 2. 183–4). He is literally an excommunicate, denying any spiritual or psychic basis for a human community. His analogue, in another kind of play, is Thersites, and in yet another, Iago. In this play simply the thing he is shall make him live. Like Mak, in *The Second Shepherds' Play*, as well as Parolles in *All's Well That Ends Well*, he constitutes a condition that is antithetical to the processes by which men and societies become whole. Like Mak and Parolles also, he is forgiven, though less as a promise of his own regeneration than as a signification of the power of charity. In Lucio's case forgiveness is grudging, but in keeping with the mode in which he is represented throughout, it is also amusing. We know what is in store for him during most of the play, and the moment when he unhoods the Duke is a rich fulfilment of comic expectation and pleasure. "This may prove worse than hanging" (V. 1. 358), he says immediately, and in his terms it does. Significantly, the Duke leaves his sentence for the very last, and Lucio remains on stage for the whole of the final scene, modulating its seriousness with his own farcical discomfiture. When his turn comes, the Duke first says that he "cannot pardon" him, but the Duke's tone, if not his language, is clearly playful:

> You, sirrah, that knew me for a fool, a coward,
> One all of luxury, an ass, a madman!
> Wherein have I so deserv'd of you
> That you extol me thus?

LUCIO: Faith, my lord, I spoke it but according to the trick. If you will hang me for it, you may; but I had rather it would please you I might be whipt.

DUKE: Whipt first, sir, and hang'd after.
> Proclaim it, Provost, round about the city,
> If any woman wrong'd by this lewd fellow –
> As I have heard him swear himself there's one
> Whom he begot with child, let her appear,
> And he shall marry her. The nuptial finish'd,
> Let him be whipt and hang'd.

LUCIO: I beseech your Highness, do not marry me to a whore. Your Highness said even now I made you a duke; good my lord, do not recompense me in making me a cuckold.

DUKE: Upon mine honour, thou shalt marry her.
> Thy slanders I forgive; and therewithal
> Remit thy other forfeits. Take him to prison;
> And see our pleasure herein executed.

LUCIO: Marrying a punk, my lord, is pressing to death, whipping, and hanging.

DUKE: Slandering a prince deserves it.

(V. 1. 498)

The entire sequence is a consummate blend of comedy and seriousness, and Lucio leaves the stage, as he entered it, a perfect instrument of the play's peculiar tragicomic pitch.

*Measure for Measure* maintains this pitch, I think, in all its scenes, even, to an extent, in those that are clearly serious. The three celebrated scenes of the early acts, for example – the two between Angelo and Isabella and the one between her and Claudio – are passionate and compelling, but they seem at the same time calculated, in performance, to circumscribe the tragic possibilities they portray. The first meeting between Angelo and Isabella, witnessed by both Lucio and the Provost, is cast essentially as a debate in which we respond to the emerging feelings of the participants at least in part as complex exemplifications of two trains of thought, theirs and Shakespeare's; and though we necessarily become involved in the feelings themselves, Lucio's role in the scene as Isabella's sardonic prompter acts as a further restraint. The second scene between Isabella and Angelo has no witnesses and is perhaps for that reason the most unsettling, but it too partly calls attention to itself as a debate, and, in addition, for all its brutality, has more than a tincture of humor, because until virtually the end Isabella remains unviolated even by Angelo's words. She simply cannot understand him; and on stage, at least, this inflection of her innocence has a comic as well as serious cadence. There is, finally, a similar humor in the scene between her and Claudio that the Duke observes, a scene in which the gravity of Claudio's feelings is at once intensified and tempered by the adolescent transparency of hers. Again, in the theater, the combination of sympathy and incipient amusement in our response to Isabella is unmistakable and, even for a director bent on dark thoughts, difficult to suppress.

Beyond such subtle controls, however, beyond the comedy of Lucio and the subplot, beyond all else in the play, it is the Duke who is most responsible for setting the tone and determining the nature of our response. We learn at the outset of the drama, in the third scene, that he is remaining in Vienna to observe and control a situation he has deliberately contrived as a trial, and we are subsequently never allowed to forget either his presence or his power. He is kept before our eyes in a brief scene (II. 3), otherwise unnecessary for the plot, that is interposed between the two meetings of Angelo and Isabella, and he is actually on stage observing the entire scene between Isabella and Claudio in prison. We therefore wonder not if he will intervene, but when and how. We expect his intervention (the whole plot of the play constitutes an intervention), and this expectation alone suggests that the modern notion of the play's division between incompatible modes of fact and fiction is a falsification.[30] In the theater, our pervasive anticipation of the Duke's reentry into the action, combined with the nature of his overt stage management later in the play, creates a unified, if highly sophisticated, effect. It necessarily disengages us to some extent from the action, even in the early scenes, and modulates our response to potentially tragic situations. We watch Claudio and Angelo not only with the Duke, but in large measure through his eyes, and no matter how much they may suffer, we are always conscious that they are actors in a drama he has contrived for their ultimate benefit. At the same time, because his active intervention is delayed, and by no means omnipotent when it comes, our feelings are deliberately involved in the action. Both Shakespeare and the Duke give Isabella, Claudio, and Angelo the scope to develop their emotions with an intensity that moves us as well as them. The result, as Walter Pater wrote, is that the play "remains a comedy, as is indeed congruous with the bland, half-humourous equity which informs the whole composition . . . yet it is hardly less full of what is really tragic in man's existence than if Claudio had indeed 'stooped to death.' "[31]

The form that such a conjunction of responses describes is in fact tragicomedy, and in *Measure for Measure* Shakespeare gives that form a radical expression. Guarini had written that

He who composes tragicomedy takes from tragedy its great persons but not its great action, its verisimilar plot but not its true one, its movement of the feelings but not its disturbance of them, its pleasure but not its sadness, its danger but not its death; from comedy it takes laughter that is not excessive, modest amusement, feigned difficulty, happy reversal, and above all the comic order.[32]

*Measure for Measure* conforms to this definition fairy closely and shares with Shakespeare's other tragicomedies a number of distinctive developments of the pattern it describes.[33] It is exceptionally self-conscious, calling constant attention to its theatricality, not only late in the play but at the start, and it is deliberately designed to translate our awareness of theatrical artifice into a consciousness of transcendent forces in human life. The Duke truly moves through the play simultaneously "like power divine" and like a stage director, an analogy that does not require us to see him as an allegorical representation of Christ, but that does encourage us to associate the dynamics of the play itself with a providential psychological and spiritual process. In this respect the patent theatricality of the ending is less an evasion of the play's serious ideas than a fulfilment of them. We have watched the play throughout both from the wings and the stalls, and, in a paradox that is familiar in many of Shakespeare's plays but especially germane to this one, we are made to understand that what seems illusory is finally most real: that the "after-dinner's sleep" and the "seeming" are part of the earlier experiences of Angelo, Isabella, and Claudio, and that the deeper truth of their lives is the Duke's fiction.[34]

*Measure for Measure* also, like Shakespeare's other tragicomedies, has a generically appropriate overall effect. There is no sense, of course, of the epiphanies of the last plays, and perhaps not even of the wonder that characterizes *All's Well That Ends Well*. *Measure for Measure* has no miraculous cures, and the distance between Helena's vulnerable passion and the Duke's combination of dispassion and charitable concern is considerable. But the play is nevertheless not without marvelousness, and its own miracles are not less great because we are aware of how they have been contrived. It remains a marvel, both theatrically and idealogically, that the punishment not only fits but transforms the crime, that mercy can eventually be consistent with justice, and that each of the characters in the play can be meted a measure as good as it is exact. Moreover, both the language and action repeatedly reveal the wonder of regenerated life, not only literally, as character after character is reprieved from death, but more profoundly, as death itself becomes understood as a part of life and as the desire for life is progressively illuminated by the kind of charity that culminates in Isabella's remarkable plea for the life of Angelo.

This understanding and these paradoxes, of course, are those of Christian experience itself, and in *Measure for Measure,* as in his other tragicomedies, Shakespeare identifies the form of the play with the shape of the life it represents. The Duke speaks explicitly of making "heavenly comforts of despair" (IV. 3. 106), and the idea of *felix culpa* clearly animates the psychic as well as spiritual movement of the play.[35] The action describes an arc that moves almost dialectically from tragic to comic possibilities: literally from the fear of death to the joy of anticipated marriage, from destructive repression to creative expression, from imprisonment to freedom, from sin to grace. In few other plays in the canon, except the final romances, is the pattern of *felix culpa* more encompassing or more deep. Tragic experience is not merely the prelude to comic salvation in *Measure for Measure* but its precondition, the means by which it can be understood and achieved: "For els how can my sinnes be forgiven me, without I felt them and knowledged them."

The distinction of *Measure for Measure* among Shakespeare's other tragicomedies, I think, is that these antinomies and paradoxes are extraordinarily acute, and their resolution difficult, not only for the characters, but for us as well. The Duke is no Prospero, though he may resemble him, and the play is not entirely his, though he sets it in motion and eventually sets it right. The human nature that is at once the subject and material of his drama is fallen and sometimes intractable. Because he delays his intervention, his actors overplay their roles, beyond even his expectation, and create painful problems, and when he does actively intervene, they will not stick to his script. He must

exert himself, and so must we.[36] To an extent that is thus unusual in tragicomedy, we ourselves are not only drawn into the
action, but implicated in it: the degree to which we are entan-
gled by Isabella, Claudio, and Angelo is a measure of our own
necessarily mortal condition, and our hope for their comic deliverance is an extension of the capacity for hope and forgiveness in our own lives. We experience, we do not merely observe, the process by which they are brought to self-knowledge
and regeneration: what the Duke's play is for them, Shakespeare's is for us. Thus, to paraphrase Pater, "the action of the
play, like the action of life itself for the keener observer," develops in us not only the conception of charity, but the "yearning to realise it."[37]

# 5

# All's Well That Ends Well

Most critics of *All's Well That Ends Well* seem to be agreed that, like *Measure for Measure*, it suffers from an inability to unify or assimilate its own material.[1] The most obvious problem is Bertram. In Boccaccio, Beltramo is simply an aristocrat, who is presented sparely and casually. He has the King's sympathy in being required to marry Giletta, and we see his rejection of her, as well as the assignment of the task, as a function of the story rather than of his character. The harsh implications of his action are muted. Shakespeare insists, as his source does not, upon Bertram's unpleasantness and deceitfulness. His contemptuous response to Helena's suit is deliberately contrasted to that of the other young lords whom the King offers to her; his refusal to kiss her when they part is gratuitously unkind; and the way in which he speaks of or to her is cruel: "Here comes my clog" (II. 5. 52), " 'Till I have no wife, I have nothing in France" (III. 2. 72). His mother, in the middle of the play, says that "his sword can never win / The honour that he loses" (III. 2. 92), and at the end he appears to lose even the honor his sword has won. He squirms and lies under Diana's accusations and seems at his most unattractive precisely at the moment he is being redeemed.

That Helena should have to suffer such a man, and more, that she should choose to love him, are of course the real problems of the play, and Shakespeare does not allow us to resolve them simply by treating them as conventions and thereby ignoring them. Helena is too warm, in her expression as in her conception, and too alert to her own predicament for us to be able simply to dismiss the obvious disproportion between her and

Bertram. Where he seems a selfish child, she is a woman; where he is coarse grained, she is sensitive; and where he is unprepared for love, she seems its creature and its emblem. The painfulness of these dichotomies is continually forced upon our consciousness not only by the commentaries of characters like the King, Lafeu, and the Countess, but by the responses of Helena herself. She is no Giletta, still less a Griselda, and her story is not one that such analogues would explain. She feels too much, and we are a witness to those feelings. She may behave like her clever folk prototypes in eventually fulfilling the tasks that her husband commands of her, but she does not easily accommodate herself to the animus behind the commands – as she says, " 'Tis bitter" (III. 2. 73) – nor does she easily forget her experience in obeying them:

> O strange men!
> That can such sweet use make of what they hate,
> When saucy trusting of the cozen'd thoughts
> Defiles the pitchy night. So lust doth play
> With what it loathes, for that which is away.
>
> (IV. 4. 21)

The eventual result of such speeches and of the predicaments that give rise to them can be a sense that Helena is being abused not only by Bertram but by Shakespeare as well. She seems, at times, a creature from another kind of play, too richly endowed both for her husband and for the plot in which she is called upon to act; so that the part she does in fact perform, and her consciousness of it, come uncomfortably close to making her seem either a fool or a knave, though clearly she is neither.

There are, moreover, other symptoms in *All's Well* of a similar sense of disproportion and "strain."[2] Throughout the play, for example, there seems to be an opposition between realistic and romantic motives. Lavache's "foul-mouth'd" calumnies have an ironic, if not satiric, bias that can appear not merely to parody Helena's quest but to depreciate it. Parolles's characterization, though intelligible enough in terms of a morality play – he is the word where Helena is the deed of honor, Bertram's vice where she is the virtue – has seemed to many critics to be at odds with the expressive mode in which Helena herself exists. The scenes of his exposure, in particular, have a dissonant and distinctly Jonsonian ring. The play as a whole appears to raise moral issues – the nature of honor most especially – that seem both inadequately expressed and summarily resolved in the action itself. Like Helena's relationship to Bertram, the action and the ideas it contains appear disjoined, and never more so than in the play's ending. A theatrically self-indulgent *scène à faire,* the last scene, like its counterpart in *Measure for Measure,* appears not so much to resolve the intellectual and emotional issues of the play as to circumvent them.

The majority of critics have tried to cope with these problems, and others like them, by in effect emphasizing one element or impulse in the play at the expense of another. Thus, some have stressed the conventional romantic and folkloristic nature of Helena's difficulties, whereas others have insisted upon the satire in the play and the intractability of much of its material to romantic treatment.[3] Precisely because each of these views is justified, however, neither is alone sufficient to establish the play's integrity. Helena's tasks (and solutions) are no doubt conventional, but their tradition hardly explains the abrasive ways in which Shakespeare actually depicts them; and though there is much in the play that is foul mouthed and calumnious, its overall configuration is demonstrably romantic and gracious. Clearly, an intepretation of the play that can unite these apparent contradictions would have the merit of arguing from rather than against the play's peculiar composition and would offer a possibility of granting it the kind of success that it can, in fact, achieve on stage.

The first step is to recognize that, like *Measure for Measure,* the play is a tragicomedy and that its various disjunctions are deliberate and part of a pervasive and self-consciously paradoxical conception. The very nature of love in the play, as Shaw saw, is paradoxical. The sexual roles are almost completely inverted: the woman pursues the man, chastity becomes the aggressor, the gentle female assumes the offensive. *All's Well* is a *Taming of the Shrew* in reverse, and from the perception of this fundamental paradox the play proliferates a host of others. Helena is at once sexually aggressive and feminine, Bertram at once passive and masculine. Her actions are instances both of her own and a transcendent will, whereas his have a value and effect quite contrary to what he supposes. Unlike his companion Parolles, whose word of honor never becomes the deed, Bertram's deed of dishonor eventually becomes the word and act of honor.

Not only the action of the play, moreover, but its language and imagery are suffused with paradox. In the very first scene (in an important dialogue to which I shall return) Helena and Parolles debate the topic of virginity, Helena attempting to discover, at more than one level, "how virgins might blow up men," while Parolles descants bawdily upon variations of how "Virginity being blown down, man will quicklier be blown up" (I. 1. 115). The debate, itself paradoxical, is a precise reflection and forecast of Helena's paradoxical predicament, and it ends with a speech by Helena that is composed totally of paradoxes. She describes to Parolles the love that Bertram shall have in the Court:

> There shall your master have a thousand loves,
> A mother, and a mistress, and a friend.
> A phoenix, captain, and an enemy,
> A guide, a goddess, and a sovereign,
> A counsellor, a traitress, and a dear;
> His humble ambition, proud humility,
> His jarring concord, and his discord dulcet,
> His faith, his sweet disaster; and with a world
> Of pretty, fond, adoptious cristendoms
> That blinking Cupid gossips.
>
> (I. 1. 154)

This speech can be puzzling in its immediate context, but all of its paradoxical collocations are eventually enacted by Helena in her pursuit of Bertram, especially in the consummation of the bedtrick itself.

Shortly after her debate with Parolles, Helena talks to the

Countess of her love for Bertram in similarly paradoxical terms,
pleading that if the Countess

> Did ever in so true a flame of liking
> Wish chastely and love dearly that your Dian
> Was both herself and Love; O, then, give pity
> To her whose state is such that cannot choose
> But lend and give where she is sure to lose;
> That seeks not to find that her search implies,
> But, riddle-like, lives sweetly where she dies!

(I. 3. 202)

Similar riddles, all of them associated with Helena, abound in
the play. In arguing that the King should trust to her cure,
Helena tells him that

> Great floods have flown
> From simple sources, and great seas have dried
> When miracles have by the greatest been denied.
> Oft expectation fails, and most oft there
> Where most it promises; and oft it hits
> Where hope is coldest, and despair most fits.

(II. 1. 138)

Bertram writes to Helena that until he has *"no wife"* he has
*"nothing in France,"* and upon the report of her death two lords
use similar paradoxes to describe the inversion of Bertram's values:

1 LORD: I am heartily sorry that he'll be glad of this.
2 LORD: How mightily sometimes we make us comforts of our losses!
1 LORD: And how mightily some other times we drown our gain in
tears! The great dignity that his valour hath here acquir'd for
him shall at home be encount'red with a shame as ample.

(IV. 3. 60)

Helena contrives a plot with the widow,

> which, if it speed,
> Is wicked meaning in a lawful deed,
> And lawful meaning in a lawful act;
> Where both not sin, and yet a sinful fact.

(III. 7. 44)

Bertram boasts to Diana that "A heaven on earth I have won by wooing thee," and she replies, after his exit, "For which live long to thank both heaven and me! / You may so in the end.... in this disguise, I think't no sin / To cozen him that would unjustly win" (IV. 2. 66, 67-8, 75-6). As the play draws to a close, Helena twice assures the Widow (and us) that "the time will bring on summer, / When briers shall have leaves as well as thorns / And be as sweet as sharp.... All's Well That Ends Well" (IV. 4. 31-3, 35; V. 1. 25); and that end is itself revealed in a cascade of riddling paradoxes. When the King asks Diana why she has apparently wrongfully accused Bertram, she answers:

> Because he's guilty, and he is not guilty.
> He knows I am no maid, and he'll swear to't:
> I'll swear I am a maid, and he knows not.
>         ... for this lord
> Who hath abus'd me as he knows himself,
> Though yet he never harm'd me, here I quit him.
> He knows himself my bed he hath defil'd;
> And at that time he got his wife with child.
> Dead though she be, she feels her young one kick;
> So there's my riddle: one that's dead is quick –
> And now behold the meaning.
>
>       *Re-enter* WIDOW *with* HELENA
>
>                       (V. 3. 282)

The preoccupation with riddles, oxymorons, and paradoxical oppositions is conventional in tragicomedy and an outgrowth of its basic pattern. According to the theory and practice of both Guarini and Fletcher the theatricality of a tragicomedy is a function of its capacity to accentuate and juxtapose the bitter and the sweet, and understood on this basis alone *All's Well* is more intelligible than many critics have found it. However, at the same time that Shakespeare unquestionably exploits this theatrical capital, he is also interested in exploring its deeper implications, and at this level his use of tragicomic form becomes even more significant and the play itself more interesting.

The basic pattern of tragicomedy, as both Guarini and Fletcher defined it – and as it was in fact practiced by English

coterie dramatists like Marston, even in ostensible comedies –
placed primary stress not simply upon a mixture of comedy and
tragedy but upon an action that came to a comic resolution despite or even because of its tragic possibilities; as Fletcher wrote,
"A tragie-comedie is not so called in respect of mirth and killing,
but in respect it wants deaths, which is inough to make it no
tragedie, yet brings some neere it, which is inough to make it no
comedie."[4] For Fletcher this pattern became an end in itself, a
means of creating and sustaining peripeties of action and mood,
but for Guarini the pattern became a theatrical expression of the
paradox of the fortunate fall[5] – and, as in *Measure for Measure*, it
is this paradox, with its rich reverberations, that eventually crystallizes all the others in *All's Well That Ends Well*.

Whether Shakespeare was following Guarini's example directly in exploring the idea of *felix culpa* in his tragicomedies and
romances or whether, independently, he discovered it to be
implicit within the conventions of the form, it affects *All's Well*
profoundly. The King refers to it directly in the closing lines of
the play:

> All yet seems well; and if it end so meet,
> The bitter past, more welcome is the sweet;
>
> (V. 3. 326)

but it is also inherent in the action. An ultimately beneficent
Providence is a central protagonist of the play, and Helena
throughout is explicitly associated with it, acting as its instrument and agent. She tells the Countess that the receipt from her
father by which she hopes to cure the King "Shall for my legacy
be sanctified / By th' luckiest stars in heaven" (I. 3. 236–7), and
when she persuades the King that "great floods have flown /
From simple sources," her root paradox is that

> He that of greatest works is finisher
> Oft does them by the weakest minister.
>
> (II. 1. 135)

The King's cure is itself described as " 'A Showing of a Heavenly
Effect in an Earthly Actor' " (II. 3. 23), and from that time for-

ward Helena bears the insignia of a power that can transform
sickness into health and sorrow into joy. After the Countess
learns that Bertram has deserted her, she exclaims:

> What angel shall
> Bless this unworthy husband? He cannot thrive,
> Unless her prayers, whom heaven delights to hear
> And loves to grant, reprieve him from the wrath
> Of greatest justice.
>
> (III. 4. 25)

Helena herself assures the Widow that she should

> Doubt not but heaven
> Hath brought me up to be your daughter's dower,
> As it hath fated her to be my motive
> And helper to a husband.
>
> (IV. 4. 18)

Throughout *All's Well*, therefore, our responses to Helena and
to the action that she generates are affected by our awareness of
the transcendental force that is working through them, and this
awareness allows us at once to submit to the multiple paradoxes
of the play and to stand above them, perceiving the pattern that
they compose. Tragicomedy conventionally demands such a
"middle mood" to assure us that the outcome will be comic and
to enable us to appreciate its artifice. In *All's Well*, Shakespeare,
like Guarini before him, was stimulated to relate this formal
requirement to an understanding of experience itself.

In Shakespeare, as we would expect, this understanding is
developed in ways and to a degree that are only suggested in *Il
Pastor Fido* and its successors, though the initial dramatic premises remain the same. To begin with, Shakespeare saw the extent to which the tragicomic dramatist could convert the audience's consciousness of the artifice of the playwright into an
awareness of the artifice of Providence and thereby associate the
workings of Providence with the dynamics of the play itself.
This is a development that finds more obvious expression in
plays like *Measure for Measure* and *The Tempest*, where the Duke
and Prospero act simultaneously "like power divine" and like

theatrical producers, but it is evident in *All's Well*, too. Helena directs a script for which she is at least in part responsible, and the last act especially is designed to make us conscious of the congruence of her theatrical and transcendental powers. Understood in this way, its obvious contrivance is a natural extension of the action of the play rather than a falsification or evasion of it. The very acuteness of the paradoxes that surround Helena, as well as her constant association with a force larger than herself, have compelled us from the start to remain at some distance from the action, and the last scene simply turns this sense of disengagement upon the play itself, enabling us to experience, rather than merely deduce, a union between the dispensations of the stage and of life.

This union, however, is hardly simple. Helena in herself is neither an Olympian playwright nor Providence, whatever reverberations of both she may generate in the play, and though she may ultimately feel assured that all will end well, that assurance insulates neither her nor us from the experience of suffering. She can work a two-day miracle upon the King, but her redemption of the man she loves takes time and pain. Even her providential assurances are complicated and qualified. At the very moment that she tells the Widow that heaven has ensured that she shall be Diana's dower, her thoughts turn to the actual experience of the bedtrick, and she cannot help meditating upon the "strange men, / That can such sweet use make of what they hate." And this paradox returns us to Bertram, in whose characterization all the paradoxes of form and substance in the play find their sharpest, and for many critics, their most unacceptable, expression.

Dr. Johnson's dissatisfaction with Bertram is celebrated and typical:

I cannot reconcile my heart to Bertram; a man noble without generosity, and young without truth; who marries Helen as a coward, and leaves her as a profligate: when she is dead by his unkindness, sneaks home to a second marriage, is accused by a woman whom he has wronged, defends himself by falshood, and is dismissed to happiness.[6]

More recent commentaries sophisticate Johnson's attitude without essentially changing it. A. P. Rossiter, for example, acknowledges the romantic decorum of the action, but insists that Shakespeare himself deliberately violates it with his characterization of Bertram:

*Uneasiness* I consider the one real quality of the play (as it is of the endings of *Troilus and Cressida* and *Measure for Measure*). We know we should not look 'conventional' comedy-ending gift-marriages in the mouth: that there is a tide in the affairs of fifth Acts that pairs males and females off mechanically, into which further inquiry is inapposite. But the disagreeable qualities of this male have been so convincingly built up, the Beast made so unbeautifully beastly, that the effect is to shake to its fairy-tale foundations the very convention we are expected to accept.[7]

Neither Rossiter, whose complaint is ostensively aesthetic, nor Johnson, whose antipathy to Bertram is moral, takes sufficient account of the paradoxes of tragicomic form in the play, but their objections nonetheless cannot be answered by formal arguments alone. The difficulties that Bertram poses, for Helena as well as the critics, are at the heart of *All's Well*, and I think no interpretation can do justice to the play without coming to terms with them and dealing directly with the nature of Bertram's experience.

To begin with, it is important to appreciate that Bertram is quite young. Whatever the statutory age of wards of the court may have been, in the play he is presented as an egregiously adolescent boy. The Countess' son, the King's ward, Parolles's dupe, he is clearly not yet his own man. He is actually called "boy" at most of the critical turns in the action. Early in the play, Parolles simultaneously coaxes and goads him to go to war by playing upon the word:

> BERTRAM: I am commanded here and kept a coil with
>        'Too young' and 'The next year' and "Tis too early'.
> PAROLLES: An thy mind stand to 't, boy, steal away bravely.
>
>                                  (II. 1. 27)
>
> PAROLLES: To th' wars, my boy, to th' wars!
>        He wears his honour in a box unseen

That hugs his kicky-wicky here at home,
Spending his manly marrow in her arms,
Which should sustain the bound and high curvet
Of Mars's fiery steed.

(II. 3. 271)

Later, during his own exposure, Parolles repeatedly condemns
Bertram for being a boy: "a foolish idle boy, but for all that very
ruttish"; "a dangerous and lascivious boy"; "that lascivious
young boy the Count" (IV. 3. 199–200, 202–3, 277). Moreover,
both the King and the Countess call Bertram a boy, the King
when Bertram first refuses to marry Helena: "Proud scornful
boy, unworthy this good gift" (II. 3. 149), and the Countess after
he has deserted Helena: "This is not well, rash and unbridled
boy" (III. 2. 26).

These references are hardly complimentary, of course, but at
the same time that they clearly stigmatize Bertram's behavior
they also partially mitigate it. For what might seem intolerable in
a man is often at least understandable, if still unattractive, in an
adolescent boy. Johnson accuses Bertram of being "young without truth," but surely few adolescents can be truthful, either to
themselves or others, about sexual impulses that they have not
yet fully experienced and therefore cannot understand. Such
truth is hard enough for grown men. Indeed, though Bertram's
behavior is often unappetizing, critics react to him with suspi-
ciously exaggerated distaste. Johnson, elsewhere in his notes on
*All's Well*, accuses Bertram of the "double crime of cruelty and
disobedience, joined likewise with some hypocrisy,"[8] and Rossiter claims that Bertram is a "weak, cowardly, mean-spirited,
false, and ill-natured human being."[9] It seems to me that the
tone, if not the substance, of such charges is excessive and reflects a displacement of the critics' real animus, which is against
the nakedness of sexuality to which Bertram's adolescence
makes him prey. That, indeed, they apprehend accurately, but
where they turn away from it and condemn it, Shakespeare is at
once more dispassionate, more charitable, and more interesting.

In any event, I myself would argue that sexuality is the major preoccupation of the play and that, as in *Measure for Measure,* it has spiritual and psychological resonances that are realized with complex but controlled tragicomic decorum. Let me begin, however, with an apparent digression. As many critics have noticed, *All's Well* makes an insistent contrast, visually as well as verbally, between the old and the young; between a generation that is dead or dying and one that is being born; between aging people who look primarily and plangently to the past, hoping but uncertain that its values can endure, and the very young, who have little memory and are fiercely intent upon the desires of the present. The Countess initiates both the contrast and its eventual overtones in the opening words of the play: "In delivering my son from me, I bury a second husband" (I. 1. 1); and within the space of a few succeeding lines, after we learn that the King is dying, the Countess eulogizes Helena's dead father and expresses the hope that both she and Bertram will prove worthy of their inheritance. Of Helena's worth she seems already convinced:

> I have those hopes of her good that her education promises; her dispositions she inherits, which makes fair gifts fairer; for where an unclean mind carries virtuous qualities, there commendations go with pity – they are virtues and traitors too. In her they are the better for their simpleness; she derives her honesty, and achieves her goodness.
>
> (I. 1. 32)

Her benediction for Bertram as she sends him, "an unseason'd courtier," off to the King's court is less confident, but enunciates similar ideas and hopes:

> Be thou blest, Bertram, and succeed thy father
> In manners, as in shape! Thy blood and virtue
> Contend for empire in thee, and thy goodness
> Share with thy birthright!
>
> (I. 1. 54)

At court the King repeats the same feelings and thoughts in more detail and with greater intensity. His first sight of Bertram

reminds him of Bertram's father, and his words are an echo of
the Countess's:

> Youth, thou bear'st thy father's face;
> Frank nature, rather curious than in haste,
> Hath well compos'd thee. Thy father's moral parts
> Mayst thou inherit too!

A moment later, dwelling on his own age and disease, he says:

> It much repairs me
> To talk of your good father. In his youth
> He had the wit which I can well observe
> To-day in our young lords; but they may jest
> Till their own scorn return to them unnoted
> Ere they can hide their levity in honour.

Then, overwhelmed by memories and by weariness, he not only
invokes Bertram's father on the subject of youth and age, he
quotes him:

> 'Let me not live' quoth he
> 'After my flame lacks oil, to be the snuff
> Of younger spirits, whose apprehensive senses
> All but new things disdain; whose judgments are
> Mere fathers of their garments; whose constancies
> Expire before their fashions'. This he wish'd.
> I, after him, do after him wish too,
> Since I nor wax nor honey can bring home,
> I quickly were dissolved from my hive,
> To give some labourers room.
>
> (I. 2. 19–22, 30–5, 58–67)

Finally, later, when Bertram disdains to marry Helena, the King
echoes the Countess once again in a speech that has long been
recognized as a centerpiece of the play:

> Strange is it that our bloods,
> Of colour, weight, and heat, pour'd all together,
> Would quite confound distinction, yet stand off
> In differences so mighty. If she be
> All that is virtuous – save what thou dislik'st,
> A poor physician's daughter – thou dislik'st
> Of virtue for the name; but do not so.

From lowest place when virtuous things proceed,
The place is dignified by th' doer's deed;
Where great additions swell's, and virtue none,
It is a dropsied honour. Good alone
Is good without a name. Vileness is so:
The property by what it is should go,
Not by the title. She is young, wise, fair;
In these to nature she's immediate heir;
And these breed honour. That is honour's scorn
Which challenges itself as honour's born
And is not like the sire. Honours thrive
When rather from our acts we them derive
Than our fore-goers. The mere word's a slave,
Debauch'd on every tomb, on every grave
A lying trophy; and as oft is dumb
Where dust and damn'd oblivion is the tomb
Of honour'd bones indeed.

(II. 3. 116)

The ideas and feelings that are expressed in these speeches –
and particularly the association of the old with the achievement
of honour and the young with its promise or betrayal – permeate
the play, often affecting it, as we shall see, in ways that are
profound though not immediately apparent. It is therefore especially interesting that Shakespeare added these associations to
the story he found in his primary source. They are compatible
with Boccaccio's tale, but Boccaccio himself does not develop
them. In Boccaccio, youth and age are not insistently juxtaposed
and there is no concern at all with either as a spiritual or
psychological condition. The Countess does not exist, nor does
Lafeu, nor Parolles, nor Lavache; and the story lacks not only
their presence but the moral commentaries that they generate.
Even the King's role is greatly diminished: he is more Beltramo's
kinsman than his foster-father; he is "very loth" to grant Giletta's request; and once he has fulfilled that function he disappears from the story. At the end Beltramo is his own judge and
jury.

If the resonances we have been discussing are missing from
Boccaccio, however, they do appear in extremely illuminating

ways in a rather unexpected source, "Upon Some Verses of *Virgil*," the essay by Montaigne to which I referred in interpreting *Othello* and which Shakespeare almost certainly had in mind when he was composing *All's Well That Ends Well*. One passage in the essay, to which Rossiter has called attention,[10] has particularly striking parallels with some of the turns of thought in the play that we have just been examining. Montaigne speaks of the relationship between nobility (birth) and virtue and argues against those who consider them coextensive:

Indeed these things have affinitie; but therewithall great difference: their names and titles should not thus be commixt: both are wronged so to be confounded. *Nobilitie is a worthy, goodly quality, and introduced with good reason, but in as much as it dependeth on others, and may fall to the share of my vicious and worthlesse fellowe, it is in estimation farre shorte of vertue.* If it be a vertue, it is artificiall and visible; relying both on time and fortune; divers in forme, according unto countries: living and mortall: without birth, as the river *Nilus*, genealogicall and common: by succession and similitude: drawne along by consequence, but a very weake one. Knowledge, strength, goodnesse, beauty, wealth and all other qualities fall within compasse of commerce and communication: whereas this consumeth it selfe in it selfe, of no emploiment for the service of others.[11]

The similarities between this argument and the King's (and Countess's) speeches are evident enough, but what makes the passage even more suggestive is its context in Montaigne's essay, for Montaigne's immediate concern is the relationship between marriage and love – by which he means sexual desire – and his discrimination of virtue and nobility is offered as an analogue of that relationship:

A man doth not marry for himselfe, whatsoever he aleageth; but as much or more for his posteritie and familie. The use and interest of mariage concerneth our off-spring, a great way beyond us. Therefore doth this fashion please me, to guide it rather by a third hand, and by anothers sence, then our owne: All which, how much doth it dissent from amorous conventions? Nor is it other then a kinde of incest, in this reverent alliance and sacred bond, to employ the efforts and extravagant humor of an amorous licentiousness. . . .

*I see no mariages faile sooner, or more troubled, then such as are concluded for beauties sake, and hudled up for amorous desires.* There are required more solide foundations, and more constant grounds, and a more warie marching to it this earnest youthly heate serveth to no purpose. Those who thinke to honour marriage, by joyning love unto it, (in mine opinion) doe as those, who to doe vertue a favour, holde, that nobilitie is no other thing then Vertue.[12]

Montaigne then continues with the passage quoted above: "Indeed these things have affinitie; but therewithall great difference...."

Rossiter remarks that "It is at least a strange coincidence that Montaigne digressed to 'virtue and nobility' from the subject of marriage," and concludes that "If this coincidence means anything, then all one can say is that the 'marriage' question is never worked into Shakespeare's play."[13] It seems to me that quite the opposite is the case, as a careful consideration not only of the immediate context of Montaigne's digression but of the whole of the essay can show. For despite its improbable title, the essay's central "theame" – to use Montaigne's word – is "the acte of generation," a subject that he explores in ways that have constant and profound parallels in *All's Well*. The very configuration of the essay is suggestive. Montaigne begins, like the play, elegiacally, lamenting his own increasing age and reflecting upon the gap between the old and the young:

As I heretofore defended my selfe from pleasure, so I now ward my selfe from temperance: it haleth me too far back, and even to stupidity. I will now every way be master of my selfe. *Wisdome hath hir excesses, and no lesse need of moderation, then follie....* infancy looketh forward, and age backward; was it not that which *Janus* his double visage signified? yeares entraine me if they please: but backward.[14]

It is in response to the pressure of this consciousness that he then proceeds to explore the sexual imperatives that at once separate the generations and most ensure their literal, if not spiritual, continuity.

He begins by stressing, as he does in all his essays, the deep dependence of the mind upon the body:

Seeing *it is the mindes priviledge to renew and recover it selfe in old age,* I earnestly advise it to do it: let it bud, blossome, and flourish if it can, as

Misle-toe on a dead tree. I feare it is a traitor; so straightly is she clasped, and so hard doth she cling to my body, that every hand-while she forsakes me; to follow hir in hir necessities.

He then dwells on the needs of the body and the difficulty men usually have in acknowledging the problems to which they give rise. He quotes Seneca: *"Why doth no man confesse his faults? Because hee is yet in them; and to declare his dreame, is for him that is waking."* But his essential point, which he relates to his own most essential purpose as a writer, is that men must understand such "faults" and acknowledge them. One of his specific examples is specifically apposite to *All's Well:*

He that demanded *Thales Milesius,* whether he should solemnly deny his lechery; had he come to me, I would have answered him, he ought not to do it: for a ly is in mine opinion, worse then lechery. *Thales* advised him otherwise, bidding him sweare, thereby to warrant the more by the lesse. Yet was not his counsell so much the election, as multiplication of vice.

From this example, he proceeds to a larger condemnation of the inherent hypocrisy of men who deny their own nature when they seek to deny their own instincts and to present a false picture of their "maners." It is from this observation that he moves directly to the announcement of his subject: "And now to our theame. Why was the acte of generation made so naturall, so necessary and so just, seeing we feare to speake of it without shame, and exclude it from our serious and regular discourses?"[15]

Montaigne's answer is often as equivocal as the question, but his essential response is to look within himself and to acknowledge what he sees. "Others fashion man," he says at the start of another essay, "I repeat him."[16] What he repeats in "Upon Some Verses of *Virgil*" he finds alternately, and sometimes simultaneously, deplorable and creative, which is the same combination of attitudes found in *All's Well,* and on the same subject. As we have seen, he regards excessive sexual desire as a contamination of marriage. Wives are for procreation and companionship, mistresses for love. He insists that he himself, however, has taken the covenant of marriage very seriously: "A man

ought wisely to husband his liberty: but after he hath once sub-
mitted himselfe unto bondage, he is to stick unto it by the lawes
of common duty or at least enforce himselfe to keepe them.
Those which undertake that covenant to deale therein with hate
and contempt, do both injustly and incommodiously." He talks
of women's knowledge of the wiles of men who would seduce
them: "how we sue, how we wooe, how we sollicitie." He cites
St. Jerome: "*The divel's master-point lies in our loines,*" but speaks
also of the "tender, daintie, delicious joyes" that women offer,
and laments that "now-a-daies" such joys are likely to be ex-
ploited by young men who are "ungratefull," "undiscreet," and
"giddy-headed."[17] All of these reflections have obvious bearing
on the behavior of Bertram, and in the passage on the act of sex
itself that I quoted in the discussion of *Othello*, he touches upon
the root paradox not only of Bertram but of the whole play:

In al other things you may observe decorum and maintaine some decency: all other operations admit some rules of honesty: this cannot
onely be imagined, but vicious or ridiculous. See whether for example
sake, you can but find a wise or discreete proceeding in it. *Alexander*
said, that he knew himselfe mortall chiefly by this action, and by sleeping: sleepe doth stifle, and suppresseth the faculties of our soule: and
that both [devoureth] and dissipates them. Surely it is an argument not
onely of our originall corruption, but a badge of our vanity and deformity. On the one side nature urgeth us unto it having thereunto combined, yea fastned, the most noble, the most profitable, and the most
sensually-pleasing, of all her functions: and on the other suffereth us to
accuse, to condemne and to shunne it, as insolent, as dishonest, and as
lewder to blush at it, and allow, yea and to commend abstinence. *Are
not we most brutish, to terme that worke beastly which begets, and which
maketh us?*[18]

In the remainder of the essay Montaigne elaborates upon this
paradox and deepens it in ways that continually suggest modes
of experience in *All's Well That Ends Well*. One passage, typically
Janus-like in Montaigne's perception of his own old age, reads
in part like a commentary on Bertram:

*Love is not properly nor naturally in season, but in the age next unto infancy.*
. . . The shorter possession we allow it over our lives, the better for us.
Behold it's behavior. It is a prin-cock boy, who in his schoole, knows

not, how far one proceeds against all order: *study, exercise, custome and practise, are paths to insufficiency:* the novices beare all the sway; *Amor ordinem nescit, Love knowes or keepes no order.*

But the quotation from St. Jerome is as much a token of Montaigne's admiration for lost powers as a rebuke, for he then refers to the "sacred liberty" of love, and chastizes women who regard its "intelligence as absolutely spiritual, disdaining to draw into consideration the interest which all the sences have in the same. All serveth to the purpose."[19] In another passage, which indirectly recalls both the King's speech on the distinction between virtue and nobility in *All's Well* and Montaigne's explicit digression on the subject, Montaigne insists that pleasure must be a commerce, it must be given to be truly received, and that without such reciprocation sexual desire is meaningless as well as base: "It is a commerce needing relation and mutuall correspondency: other pleasures that we receive, may be requitted by recompences of different nature: but this cannot be repaid but with the very same kinde of coyne."[20] In another passage, one that anticipates Helena's speech on the strangeness of Bertram's lust, which played for that which was "away," Montaigne describes the insatiability of lechery and suggests its illusoriness: "It is not a passion meerely corporeall. *If no end be found in coveteousnesse, nor limit in ambition, assure your selfe there is nor ende nor limit in letchery.* It yet continueth after saciety: nor can any man prescribe it or end or constant satisfaction: it ever goeth beyond it's possession, beyond it's bounds."[21] Finally, in a passage that suggests perhaps the sharpest and deepest resemblance between the essay and the play, Montaigne concludes that indeed in all respects our bodies and souls are inexorably intertwined, and with them, our pleasure and pains, our virtues and vices: "*Our life consisteth partly in folly, and partly in wisedome....* May we not say, that there is nothing in us, during this earthly prison, simply corporall, or purely spirituall? and that injuriously we dismember a living man? that there is reason we should carrie our selves in the use of pleasure, at least as favourably as we do in the pangs of griefe?"[22] This is the same thought that is given voice by one of the lords in *All's Well* in his comment on Bertram's behavior in love and marriage: "The web of our life is of a mingled yarn, good and ill together. Our virtues would be proud if our faults whipt them not; and our crimes would despair if they were not cherish'd by our virtues" (IV. 3. 67).

It seems to me that though Boccaccio is the demonstrable source for the story of *All's Well That Ends Well*, it is Montaigne's essay that most illuminates the texture of experience in Shakespeare's dramatization of that story – the additional dramatis personae, the shifts of emphasis, the whole penumbra of thought and feeling in the play. The elegiac cast of *All's Well*, its pervasive opposition of age and youth, the association of that opposition with marriage and lust and with virtue and nobility, the depiction of Bertram as a "prin-cock boy . . . in season . . . in the age next unto infancy" – all these features of the play are part of the fabric of Montaigne's essay. Even more important than these specific analogues, moreover, is their common denominator, an unremitting focus upon erotic love and a consciousness of sexuality itself as a supreme instance of the mixed nature of our being. This was Montaigne's most important legacy to Shakespeare in *All's Well* and should, I think, be the most important emphasis in any interpretation of the play, for as I have already suggested, the source of most critical dissatisfaction with the play is ultimately an unwillingness to accept its sexual preoccupations. It is pointless and mischievous to construe *All's Well* as a romantic comedy and then chastize it for failing to be one. Its climax is not the promise of matrimony but the revelation of its literal consummation. *All's Well That Ends Well* indeed celebrates marriage, and in this respect differs quite significantly from Montaigne, but Shakespeare's major focus, like Montaigne's, is nonetheless upon the paradoxical nature of erotic energy itself.

This focus is most evident, of course, in the characterization of Bertram. Much of this depiction, as we have seen, is direct: Bertram is repeatedly called a lascivious boy, and he repeatedly acts like one. But the erotic significance of his role is also indirectly represented through the subtly modulated characterization of Parolles, who at once intensifies the implications of Bertram's behavior and dilates our response to him. Parolles is Bertram's companion, almost his shadow, for most of the play, and although he does not ostensively tempt him, we are clearly made to understand that he influences Bertram and that Bertram's very association with him is corrupting. The Countess speaks for everyone else in the play when she says that Parolles is

> A very tainted fellow, and full of wickedness.
> My son corrupts a well-derived nature
> With his inducement.
>
> (III. 2. 85)

Both the Widow and Diana repeat that thought in a specifically sexual context. The Widow remarks on Parolles's role as Bertram's pander: "I know that knave, hang him! one Parolles; a filthy officer he is in those suggestions for the young earl," and a few moments later, in her conversation with Helena, Diana stigmatizes him both as Bertram's antagonist and Helena's:

> HELENA:                          Which is the Frenchman?
> DIANA:                          He –
>     That with the plume; 'tis a most gallant fellow.
>     I would he lov'd his wife; if he were honester
>     He were much goodlier. Is't not a handsome gentleman?
> HELENA: I like him well.
> DIANA: 'Tis pity he is not honest. Yond's that same knave
>     That leads him to these places; were I his lady
>     I would poison that vile rascal.
> HELENA:                          Which is he?
> DIANA: That jack-an-apes with scarfs.
>
> (III. 5. 16–17, 74–82)

Most of the men in the play, Lafeu particularly, echo these sentiments about Parolles, and immediately after the conversation between Diana and Helena, two of the lords persuade Bertram to submit Parolles to the test that eventually exposes him.

Diana's reference to Parolles's "scarfs" has implications that

relate his characterization to Borachio's homily on fashion in
*Much Ado About Nothing*. Parolles's dandified dress is harped on
throughout the play, and would of course be visually conspicuous in any performance. Lafeu particularly is incensed by it and
suggests both its obvious and its deeper import. As the name
implies, Parolles is the word rather than the deed, and Lafeu
specifically warns Bertram that "there can be no kernel in this
light nut; the soul of this man is his clothes" (II. 5. 22). He is here
referring primarily to Parolles's boasts of prowess in battle, a
counterfeiting that is easily enough exposed. But Lafeu makes a
far more penetrating charge that he also associates with Parolles's clothes. In one of the number of serio-comic conversations that characterize their relationship throughout the play,
Parolles insists to Lafeu that though Bertram "is my good lord:
whom I serve above is my master." Lafeu asks, "Who? God?" to
which Parolles rejoins, "Ay, sir," and Lafeu then says, "The
devil it is that's thy master. Why dost thou garter up thy arms o'
this fashion? Dost make hose of thy sleeves? Do other servants
so? Thou wert best set thy lower part where thy nose stands" (II.
3. 239).

This comment locates the source of Parolles's energy in the
play rather exactly, and also certainly the source of Lafeu's com-
pulsive interest in him, for only a moment earlier, when Parolles
complains. "My lord, you do me most insupportable vexation,"
Lafeu answers, "I would it were hell pains for thy sake, and my
poor doing eternal; for doing I am past, as I will by thee, in what
motion age will give me leave" (II. 3. 225). Lafeu's whole relation to Parolles is yet another reverberation of Montaigne's essay, because Montaigne too is exasperated by his declining sexual powers; but in any case, Lafeu's charge against Parolles's
dress is central to the play and analogous to the King's more
generalized complaint (quoted from Bertram's father) about
"younger spirits . . . whose judgments are / Mere fathers of their
garments; whose constancies / Expire before their fashions."

As I suggested in the discussion of *Much Ado About Nothing*,
such an indictment of sexual fashion would have had an addi-

tional dimension for Elizabethans, because in the medieval drama that was their inheritance and that still impinged upon their stage, the Vices were commonly represented as dandies. Extravagance of dress particularly characterized Vices associated with adolescent temptation, though it had wider implications as well. Lust-and-Liking is "proudely apperlde in garmentes gaye" in *The World and the Child*, and New Gyse, Nowadays, and Nought are similarly "Nyse in ther a ray" in *Mankind*. Superbia in *The Castle of Perseverance*, if not dressed in clothes "Jagge[d]" for ornament "in every cost" himself, advises Humanum Genus to do so, and he interestingly links such fashionable dress with boasting; Courtly Abusyon, in a long soliloquy in Skelton's *Magnificence*, virtually defines his role in terms of his exorbitant apparel, "Beyonde all syse / Of the new gyse"; and in *Wisdom* Lucifer himself changes his clothes "& cummyth in a geyn as a goodly galont" to persuade Mind, Will, and Understanding to change their own habits and submit to the "pride," "covetyse," and "lechery" that gallantry signifies.[23] In the medieval drama, of course, Vice figures such as these were understood allegorically, as personifications of parts of mankind, psychomachic projections of mankind's own vicious inclinations. *All's Well* is not an allegory and Parolles's role cannot be explained by any single abstraction, but he nonetheless retains much of his theatrical ancestry. He personifies the vice of dishonor – and particularly the dominance of the lower part – which inhabits Bertram at the same time that, literally, he represents the kind of person Bertram, governed by that dominance, would find admirable.

Once he is understood in this way, Parolles emerges as – what in fact he always is in performance – a rich and commanding character, who has varied and subtle effects upon our response to Bertram and to the play. To begin with, to the extent that he embodies Bertram's self-centered adolescent aggressions, he helps absorb some of our antagonism to them. This function is particularly evident in the scene in which Parolles is hoodwinked and exposed, for in watching it Bertram is witnessing his own exposure, literally of his relations with Diana, figuratively of a part of himself. The scene as a whole is thus a psychic lesson for Bertram, even if he does not fully realize it, and helps prepare him and us for his own manifest exposure at the end of the play. And most important, it does so comically, because Parolles's significance in *All's Well* is determined not only by what he represents, but by the mode in which he is himself presented. For like his medieval forbears, he is essentially funny. From the first moment in the play, when we see him preening like a peacock, to the last, when he comes, out, plucked, to give his testimony against Bertram, he generates laughter. Many of his scenes – all those to do with the drum and with Lafeu – border on farce. It is instructive that for centuries performances of the play revolved completely around Parolles – Charles I wrote "Monsieur Parolles" as a subtitle in his copy of the Second Folio – and modern productions have confirmed that Parolles provides a keynote of the play and is more responsible than any other character for setting its tragicomic tone.

At the same time, Parolles's theatrical lineage makes that tone particularly complex. He does not, like the Vices, have really sinister overtones, but he does have serious ones. For all his comic routines, he remains, as Lafeu suggests, a demonstration of what is postlapsarian and intractable in human affairs; and he has an expressive life of his own in the play. The scenes in which he is exposed, as many spectators have testified, are powerful, and especially so because what is revealed is so familiar to him. Like the medieval Vices, the truth about himself does not make him free. When he is first unmasked, one of the lords remarks, "Is it possible he should know what he is, and be that he is?" (IV. 1. 41–2) and the answer that he proceeds to enact in the scene is a profound yes. After he has been repudiated by Bertram and left in disgrace by the soldiers, he – yet again like the Vices – explicitly and homiletically defends his identity for what it is, no more, no less:

> If my heart were great,
> 'Twould burst at this. Captain I'll be no more;
> But I will eat, and drink, and sleep as soft

> As captain shall. Simply the thing I am
> Shall make me live. Who knows himself a braggart,
> Let him fear this; for it will come to pass
> That every braggart shall be found an ass.
> Rust, sword; cool, blushes; and, Parolles, live
> Safest in shame. Being fool'd, by fool'ry thrive.
> There's place and means for every man alive.
>
> (IV. 3. 307)

A review of a performance of *All's Well* in the early 1950s, with Michael Hordern as Parolles, gives some idea of the theatrical amplitude of this scene:

And in the climax to this subplot, the interrogation of Parolles by the practical jokers who have ambushed and blindfolded him, every move and every tone was deft and delightful: the anxious gabbling of the numbers as he tumbles over himself to betray the military strength of his own side, the confidential becking of his interrogator in order to impart one extra titbit of lying scandal about his superior officers, the self-hugging satisfaction at getting through the interview, he thinks, so adroitly. When Parolles is finally unblindfolded, and discovers his captors to be his own comrades, Hordern managed a breathtaking transition from farce to deadly earnest. At the discovery he closed his eyes and fell straight backward into the arms of his attendants; then, as with taunts they prepare to leave him, he slithered to the ground, becoming wizened and sly on the instant, and with 'simply the thing I am shall make me live' revealed an essential meanness not only in Parolles but in human nature as a whole.[24]

Earlier in the scene, while marveling at Bertram's betrayal of his wife and apparent seduction of Diana, a lord remarks, "As we are ourselves, what things are we!" (IV. 3. 18). Parolles is a representation of the thing itself, a personification of the lowest common denominator of human nature, the very emblem of the corporeal demands of which Montaigne speaks in his essay. Like Bertram, whose lust (and folly) he symbolizes, Parolles is eventually accommodated in the gracious scheme of the play; Lafeu, the one person besides Helena who knew and knows him best, takes pity on him: "Sirrah, inquire further after me... Though you are a fool and a knave, you shall eat" (V. 2.

48). But as with Bertram himself this accommodation is neither easy nor pat Parolles stands in the play as a perpetual point of reference, an embodiment of the irreducible human material that informs and qualifies all miracles.

In *All's Well* those miracles are performed by Helena, and it is hardly an accident that within a few moments of the play's opening she should be engaged in a debate with Parolles and that the subject of their debate should be patently sexual. The scene repays detailed study. After bewailing her hopeless love for Bertram in a soliloquy in which she chastizes her own "ambition," Helena looks off stage and says:

Who comes here?

*Enter* PAROLLES

[*Aside*] One that goes with him. I love him for his sake;
And yet I know him a notorious liar,
Think him a great way fool, solely a coward;
Yet these fix'd evils sit so fit in him
That they take place when virtue's steely bones
Looks bleak i' th' cold wind; withal, full oft we see
Cold wisdom waiting on superfluous folly.

(I. 1. 92)

This speech is difficult, but it has affinities with the comment with which Montaigne begins his own examination of the realities of human sexuality: "*Wisedome hath hir excesses, and no lesse need of moderation, then follie.*" We do not yet know Parolles, and Helena's speech has proleptic force, because she anticipates the reasons both for his exposure and his eventual accommodation; but what we can apprehend at the moment she utters her words, I think, is that in loving Parolles for Bertram's sake she is coming to terms not simply with Bertram's companion, but with Bertram himself, and especially that part of him of which Parolles becomes so obvious a projection: the prin-cock youth with the energies of the age next unto infancy.

If there were any doubt about these implications, they are cleared up when Parolles immediately asks, "Are you meditating on virginity?" and Helena, with a forthrightness that embarrassed her Victorian critics and has unsettled a good number of her modern ones, answers, "Ay," and proceeds to engage him in a rather business-like conversation on the subject. "You have some stain of soldier in you; let me ask you a question. Man is enemy to virginity; how may we barricado it against him?" After an exchange of military metaphors, the tenor of their talk shifts:

PAROLLES: Loss of virginity is rational increase; and there was never virgin got till virginity was first lost. That you were made of is metal to make virgins. Virginity by being once lost may be ten times found; by being ever kept, it is ever lost. 'Tis too cold a companion; away with't.

HELENA: I will stand for't a little, though therefore I die a virgin.

PAROLLES: There's little can be said in't; 'tis against the rule of nature. To speak on the part of virginity is to accuse your mothers; which is most infallible disobedience. He that hangs himself is a virgin; virginity murders itself, and should be buried in highways, out of all sanctified limit, as a desperate offendress against nature. Virginity breeds mites, much like a cheese; consumes itself to the very paring, and so dies with feeding his own stomach. Besides, virginity is peevish, proud, idle, made of self-love, which is the most inhibited sin in the canon. Keep it not; you cannot choose but lose by't. Out with't. Within ten year it will make itself ten, which is a goodly increase; and the principal itself not much the worse. Away with't.

HELENA: How might one do, sir, to lose it to her own liking?

PAROLLES: Let me see. Marry, ill to like him that ne'er it likes. 'Tis a commodity will lose the gloss with lying; the longer kept, the less worth. Off with't while 'tis vendible; answer the time of request.... Will you anything with it?

(I. 1. 103–7, 122–46, 151–2)

Helena answers, "Not my virginity yet," and though a subsequent line or two seem to be missing from the text, it is clear that her mind then directly turns to the subject that has been subsuming her thought all along, for with a cascade of oxymorons to match Parolles's paradoxes, she makes her riddling speech about the paradoxical love Bertram will find in his journey to court. As the tempo of the exchange drops, she gently, though pointedly, rebukes Parolles for his cowardice, and Parolles leaves the stage with the taunt, "Get thee a good husband, and use him as he uses thee." Helena responds with a soliloquy whose mood is the very reverse of the one with which she began the scene:

> Our remedies oft in ourselves do lie,
> Which we ascribe to heaven. The fated sky
> Gives us free scope; only doth backward pull
> Our slow designs when we ourselves are dull.
> What power is it which mounts my love so high,
> That makes me see, and cannot feed mine eye?
> The mightiest space in fortune nature brings
> To join like likes, and kiss like native things.
> Impossible be strange attempts to those
> That weigh their pains in sense, and do suppose
> What hath been cannot be. Who ever strove
> To show her merit that did miss her love?
> The King's disease - my project may deceive me,
> But my intents are fix'd, and will not leave me.
>
> (I. 1. 202)

Helena's eventual cure of the King is proclaimed a miracle and is explicitly associated - as we have seen she herself is throughout the play - with a providential power greater than her own, but the human manifestation of this power, as her conversation with Parolles suggests, and as both she and we come increasingly to understand, is the creativeness as well as procreativeness of her erotic energy. It is significant that when Lafeu first introduces her to the King, he pointedly alludes to her sexual potency:

> Nay, come your ways;
> This is his Majesty; say your mind to him.
> A traitor you do look like; but such traitors
> His Majesty seldom fears. I am Cressid's uncle,
> That dare leave two together.
>
> (II. 1. 93)

Helena's sexuality, of course, unlike Cressida's, unlike her own Grecian namesake's, is beneficent and regenerative, harmonizing human society rather than destroying it. She restores the King to health, and the sexual suggestiveness of her renewal both of him and the kingdom – "Lustig, as the Dutchman says" (II. 3. 38) – has immediate intimations of "great power, great transcendance" (II. 3. 31).

Helena's sexual rejuvenation of the King is figurative. Her sexual cure of Bertram, of course, is not. Indeed, almost exactly in the manner of the Duke's cure of Angelo in *Measure for Measure*, it is homeopathic in its literalness, and as in that play it is associated deeply with the parable of the talents. Parolles points the way for Helena, at once exemplifying the essential problem in his debate with her and unintentionally indicating its solution. His comic banter about her virginity is casually obscene but, as with Lucio's memorable lines on pregnancy, the unconscious accent of his speech is a celebration not of fornication but of human generation and creativity. The metamorphosis of his libertine argument is inherent in its imagery. His speeches to Helena are suffused with usurous images that eventually suggest to her, if not to him, the true coin to be made of her virgin "metal," the profit to be realized from her sexual capital. And in a paradox that Montaigne's essay can help us appreciate, she responds to the spiritual subtext of Parolles's argument by understanding its corporeal burden: "Get thee a good husband, and use him as he uses thee." In that night in Florence, she does so. She resorts to the remedy that lies deepest within herself. To paraphrase the Geneva gloss to the parable of the talents, she continues in the knowledge of God, and does good with those graces that God has given her. She invests the talent of her virginity, thereby transforming Bertram's use of her into the fullest erotic promise of marriage.

The transformation is not easy, however, and as in *Measure for Measure* there is a deep impulse in the play to make us apprehend its difficulty rather sharply. Helena's own memory of her night with Bertram is particularly vexing, and it lingers. She

says to the Widow, in the speech from which I have already
partially quoted:

> Doubt not but heaven
> Hath brought me up to be your daughter's dower,
> As it hath fated her to be my motive
> And helper to a husband. But, O strange men!
> That can such sweet use make of what they hate,
> When saucy trusting of the cozen'd thoughts
> Defiles the pitchy night. So lust doth play
> With what it loathes, for that which is away.

(IV. 4. 18)

These are not comforting lines, and to critics like Rossiter they
seem profoundly unsettling, evidence of the play's "ambivalence" about its tale of Beauty and the Beast. But much depends
on how the lines would be spoken, which in turn depends upon
how they are construed. It seems to me that the accent is not on
horror or revulsion, but on strangeness, and that what Helena
most feels and expresses is a sense of paradoxical wonder, the
sense most appropriate to tragicomic experience. The paradoxes
are evident in the impulse of the whole of the speech: that
heaven should work through such carnal means; as well as in its
parts: that a man can make such sweet use of a woman he hates,
that his lust can so easily be satisfied by imagining she is some-
one else. The deeper paradox of Helena's lines, however, is that
though they insist on the reality of her experience of Bertram's
use, their imagery also suggests Montaigne's argument that
sexual appetite alone is an illusion, an illusion of the mind as
well as the senses. It is extremely interesting, therefore, that her
speech should be immediately preceded by the exposure of
Parolles, Bertram's psychomachic (and specifically phallic) extension, for Parolles, whose soul is his clothes, is the embodiment of the paradox that Helena finds so strange a man who is
in a sense nothing but an illusion, who knows it, and who yet
insists upon his own undeniable being. In substance and tone,
"Simply the thing I am shall make me live" is of a piece with
Helena's lines. Her wonderment at Bertram's lust is a modulation of the spectacle of Parolles's very existence.

This sense of wonder is considerably amplified and enlarged immediately following Helena's speech in a scene at Rousillon in which Lafeu ruminates on Helena and Bertram and then, in an apparent digression, turns to an examination of Lavache, the play's bittersweet clown:

CLOWN: At your service.
LAFEU: No, no, no.
CLOWN: Why, sir, if I cannot serve you, I can serve as great a prince as you are.
LAFEU: Who's that? A Frenchman?
CLOWN: Faith, sir, 'a has an English name; but his fisnomy is hotter in France than there.
LAFEU: What prince is that?
CLOWN: The Black Prince, sir; alias, the Prince of Darkness; alias, the devil.
LAFEU: Hold thee, there's my purse. I give thee not this to suggest thee from thy master thou talk'st of; serve him still.
CLOWN: I am a woodland fellow, sir, that always loved a great fire; and the master I speak of ever keeps a good fire. But, sure, he is the prince of the world; let his nobility remain in's court. I am for the house with the narrow gate, which I take to be too little for pomp to enter. Some that humble themselves may; but the many will be too chill and tender; and they'll be for the flow'ry way that leads to the broad gate and the great fire.

(IV. 5. 30)

The point of Lavache's speech, as Northrop Frye remarks, "is structural: it sums up the blind and deluded movement that sent Bertram out to the wars, and anticipates the completion of the action by which Helena brings him home again, in opposition to everything he thinks he wants."[25] Its reference to the Gospels also, as Frye indicates, gives a sudden glimpse into an order of experience outside normal human consciousness. In this respect it resembles Borachio's homily on sexual fashion and the Duke's speech on death, both of which compel us (and in *Measure for Measure* Claudio also) to disengage our attention from the material body of the action to consider the deeper forces that inform it. In *All's Well* this disengagement has particular emphasis because its point is not merely stated, but dramatized in the two preceding scenes. Lavache's speech directly follows Helena's meditative soliloquy on her night in Florence and Parolles's on his exposure All three in succession occupy barely five minutes of stage time and would form a visual and verbal palimpsest in an Elizabethan production. Together, I think, they create, in action, a perspective that dilates Bertram's specific sexual drive into an image suggesting the extraordinary and ultimately mysterious paradoxes of all human erotic energy.

Lavache's whole characterization is directed to these mysteries. "Wilt thou ever be a foul-mouth'd and calumnious knave?" the Countess asks him at the start of the play, and he answers, "A prophet I, madam; and I speak the truth the next way" (I. 3. 53). The truths he speaks in that way are generally about man's bodily condition, they are those of the Bible, and they consistently parallel the erotic action We are first introduced to him shortly after Helena resolves to follow Bertram to the King's court and just before she is obliged to make her love and her plans known to the Countess. Lavache makes a comparable revelation of his contemplated marriage to Isbel, and his parody of Helena's situation is as evident as his parody of Scripture:

CLOWN: 'Tis not unknown to you, madam, I am a poor fellow.
COUNTESS: Well, sir.
CLOWN: No, madam, 'tis not so well that I am poor, though many of the rich are damn'd; but if I may have your ladyship's good will to go to the world, Isbel the woman and I will do as we may.
COUNTESS: Wilt thou needs be a beggar?
CLOWN: I do beg your good will in this case.
COUNTESS: In what case?
CLOWN: In Isbel's case and mine own. Service is no heritage; and I think I shall never have the blessing of God till I have issue o' my body; for they say barnes are blessings.
COUNTESS: Tell me thy reason why thou wilt marry.
CLOWN: My poor body, madam, requires it. I am driven on by the flesh; and he must needs go that the devil drives.
COUNTESS: Is this all your worship's reason?

CLOWN: Faith, madam, I have other holy reasons, such as they are.
COUNTESS: May the world know them?
CLOWN: I have been, madam, a wicked creature, as you and all flesh
    and blood are; and, indeed, I do marry that I may repent.
COUNTESS: Thy marriage, sooner than thy wickedness.
CLOWN: I am out 'o friends, madam, and I hope to have friends for my
    wife's sake.
COUNTESS: Such friends are thine enemies, knave.
CLOWN: Y'are shallow, madam – in great friends; for the knaves come
    to do that for me which I am aweary of. He that ears my
    land spares my team, and gives me leave to in the crop.
    If I be his cuckold, he's my drudge. He that comforts my wife
    is the cherisher of my flesh and blood; he that cherishes my
    flesh and blood loves my flesh and blood; he that loves my
    flesh and blood is my friend; ergo, he that kisses my wife is
    my friend.

                                                              (I. 3. 13)

"Holy reasons" – the pun is on "reasons" (raisings) as well as
"holy." Even for Shakespeare the blend of obscenity and revealed truth in these lines is remarkable, but it is a mistake to
conclude that the result is an ironic depreciation either of Helena's quest or of marriage itself. On the contrary, the obscene
point is also the theological (and psychological) one, and
Lavache provides the most profound reasons both for understanding the marriage that Helena seeks and for taking it seriously. While parodying the Bible, he invokes it, and the emphasis upon the flesh that is the basis of his parody is what the
institution of marriage is designed to assimilate and make fruitful. The first purpose of marriage, according to the liturgy as
well as Lavache, is precisely the blessing of barnes, "the procreation of children," as the second is "for a remedy against sin,
and to avoid fornication" – in Lavache's words, "to repent."
Lavache also plays, of course, upon St. Paul's words in the
liturgy on the mystery of marital union: "So men are bound to
love their own wives as their own bodies. He that loveth his
own wife, loveth himself. For never did any man hate his own
flesh, but nourisheth and cherisheth it."[26]
    All of these implications are strongly inscribed in the central,

if unseen, action of *All's Well That Ends Well*, the bedtrick that
fulfills Helena's tasks and consummates her marriage to Bertram. As we have seen, Helena calls our attention to the heat of
Bertram's desire that night in Florence and to both the illusion
and reality of his pleasure, and it is the full and uninhibited
expression of desire and pleasure that makes the consummation, and with it Bertram's reclamation, both credible and mean-
ingful. Bertram rejects Helena ostensibly because she is "a poor
physician's daughter," but it is not overreading, I think, to see
behind this reason an inhibition not unlike that which both
Montaigne and Freud speak of, the feeling that Helena is his
mother's creature, virtually his sister, and therefore not a possible object of the kind of desire that drives Lavache to Isbel or
Bertram himself to Diana. Shakespeare certainly insinuates the
sense of sibling familiarity in the scene in which the Countess
exposes Helena's love by calling herself Helena's "mother,"
while Helena repeatedly protests that Bertram must not be her
"brother" (I. 3); and throughout the play Bertram is confronted
by a conspiracy of women whose nurturing affections threaten
to control and therefore deprive him of the energy of his aggressive sexual instincts, to bring him to what he calls "the dark house
and the detested wife" (II. 3. 285). The true miracle of the bedtrick, the event that condenses within itself every one of the
play's paradoxes, is that in Florence Bertram does indeed find

> A mother, and a mistress, and a friend,
> A phoenix, captain, and an enemy,
> A guide, a goddess, and a sovereign,
> A counsellor, a traitress, and a dear;
> His humble ambition, proud humility,
> His jarring concord, and his discord dulcet.
>
> (I. 1. 155)

The bedtrick resolves these many antinomies in large part because of the phoenix-like power of Helena's chastity, but also,
and fundamentally, because it releases and incorporates, rather
than denies, Bertram's aggressive sexual energies (essentially
the Parolles in him), a process of erotic experience that also

interested Shakespeare in *Measure for Measure* and whose unconscious dynamics, as we shall see, he was to explore extensively in *Cymbeline*. Bertram's freedom enables him to conquer
Helena and discover her as a woman, a conquest that provides
the basis for a marriage in which there can be desire as well as
affection and in which there is at least the prospect that he may
cherish her flesh as his own. This is the psychic reality that is
latent within the convention of the bedtrick, and Helena herself
draws our attention to it in her words of reunion with Bertram at
the end of the play: "O, my good lord, when I was like this
maid, / I found you wondrous kind" (V. 3. 303). For Elizabethans the word "kind" signified not only gentleness and
affection, but the whole range of natural human properties, specifically including the sexual function, and I think it is this
manifold sense of Bertram's "kindness," and of Helena's re-
sponsiveness to it, which allows us to accept at face value his
final vow to "love her dearly, ever, ever dearly" (V. 3. 310).

   The ending of the play, of course, is what has especially vexed
critics. Johnson, as we have seen, considered it an arbitrary and
evasive fiction, and to more recent commentators it has seemed
either unsuccessful or purposely disturbing.[27] But none of these
responses is either necessary or likely if we really attend to the
play's spiritual and psychic resonances. Some of these resonances may sound remote to us, but they are not inaccessible. If
we cannot agree with the biblical conception of fornication, we
can still appreciate its view, as well as Montaigne's, of the profound paradoxes of man's sexual nature, and once we do that,
there is nothing to prevent us from accepting Bertram and
Helena essentially in the terms in which the story offers them to
us. We may not quite be able to see Helena as a vessel of grace,
but the play certainly makes it possible for us to recognize the
power of her sexual attraction to Bertram and to sympathize
with the sanctification and profit that nature itself lends to her
procreative instinct. And if we cannot accept Bertram as the
prodigal son,[28] the play at least provides the means for us to
understand him (and Parolles) as a prodigal adolescent and an

indelible expression of our own psychological histories and condition. Moreover, these translations into modern idiom may be more of a gain than a loss, for as I suggested earlier a consciousness nurtured by twentieth-century psychological thought is perhaps closer to Shakespeare and his audience than either an evangelical Christianity like Johnson's or an agnostic Puritanism like Rossiter's.[29] It is certainly more likely to accept the inexorable and marvelous indivisibility of body and spirit, folly and wisdom, which both Montaigne and St. Paul perceived and which Shakespeare dramatizes, and it is therefore more likely to respond to *All's Well That Ends Well* with the kind of charity that animates it.

# 6

## *Cymbeline*

Informing both *Othello* and *Much Ado About Nothing* is a vision of paradise, a primary state in which body and soul are entirely harmonious and in which the mystical union of marriage is the palpable expression of psychic and spiritual integrity. Othello's whole quest is devoted to the attainment of this state of being, and in *Much Ado* its actual achievement is represented in the character of Dogberry and in his analogy with the lovers. In *Othello*, of course, this paradise is lost, and in *Much Ado* it is regained only with considerable humorous qualification, but in neither play is the idea of paradise really contradicted by experience, and both plays in fact derive tremendous energy and clarity from the celebration of innocence.

There is no comparable clarity or celebration in *Measure for Measure* and *All's Well That Ends Well*. There is no Dogberry or the possibility of one in either play: his counterparts are Lucio and Parolles, and though both are exposed and defeated, they are not, like Don John, purged from the kingdom at the end of the play, nor are they, like him, easily dismissed from memory. The Duke may eventually triumph over Lucio, but for most of the action he must put up with him, and share the stage with him, just as Helena must with Parolles; and Helena's innocence (and Isabella's) is tempered by that necessity. The plays transpire in the middle realm of tragicomedy, where characters must be tricked in bed to resolve their erotic difficulties and where erotic expression is never free, even in conception, from human imperfection.

This imperfection, moreover, extends to the social order itself. In *Much Ado* the erotic predicament of the characters clearly relates to social problems, a relationship depicted with realistic attention to manners, but the society of the play is itself untroubled: Don Pedro, significantly, though indirectly implicated in the action, is a bachelor exempt from its erotic trials. Similarly, though Othello's erotic condition has profound social components, he is barely called upon to exercise his function as a general in the play, and Venice, if not Cyprus, remains immune to his experience. In the tragicomedies, on the other hand, the health of the community is directly dependent upon the erotic health of its members. In *All's Well* the King himself is ill and in *Measure for Measure* the Duke's rule is distempered, and in each case the recuperation of the ruler is coextensive with the cure of the erotic disorder of his subjects.

As we have seen, a radical source of these disorders in both plays is the threat not merely of sexual appetite but of the narcissism and aggression it signifies, and though that threat is not entirely dispelled, it is assimilated and made fruitful in a process of moral and psychic growth that ends in marriage. Marriage is formally and substantively crucial in *All's Well* and *Measure for Measure* – it is the goal of the bedtricks, it animates the chaste energies of the heroines, and it functions at once as an ideal of erotic self-fulfillment and as an actual social institution that provides the basis for human community. But though it is still the one sanctified means of uniting sensuality and affection in the relationship of a man and a woman, and though it still signifies the communion of Christ's whole congregation, it is no longer quite experienced as an "estate, instituted of God in paradise, in the time of man's innocency" (Liturgy of Matrimony, *Book of Common Prayer*).

*Cymbeline* returns to this transcendental sense of marriage and of love at the same time that it incorporates the more mundane individual and social experiences of the problem comedies. Formally, *Cymbeline* is perhaps closest to *Much Ado About Nothing*, but it assimilates the generic characteristics and experiences of *Othello* as well as of *Measure for Measure* and *All's Well That Ends Well*; and it is no accident that in doing so, as we shall see, it resembles both the mystery drama and dreams.

Both Imogen's chastity and Posthumus's jealousy suggest the deeper erotic motifs of *Othello*. Like Desdemona's, Imogen's love for her husband is "rare" (I. 1. 135), immutable even in the face of his wish to kill her. Her devotion to Posthumus is the motive of her being, and it is especially moving in performance, where there is a visual contrast between her chaste integrity and the fantastic vicissitudes of the action to which she is subjected. The very image of her reading Posthumus's slanderous letter is affecting: "What shall I need to draw my sword?" Pisanio exclaims, "The paper / Hath cut her throat already"; and her own words suggest a sense of violation and pain not unlike Desdemona's when Othello directly abuses her as a whore:

> False to his bed? What is it to be false?
> To lie in watch there, and to think on him?
> To weep twixt clock and clock? If sleep charge nature,
> To break it with a fearful dream of him,
> And cry myself awake? That's false to's bed,
> Is't?
>
> (III. 4. 30–1, 38–42)

Later, in disguise as Fidele, answering Lucius's questions about herself and the headless body of the man she assumes to be her husband, she is even more moving:

> I am nothing; or if not,
> Nothing to be were better. This was my master,
> A very valiant Briton and a good,
> That here by mountaineers lies slain. Alas!
> There is no more such masters. I may wander
> From east to occident; cry out for service;
> Try many, all good; serve truly; never
> Find such another master.
>
> (IV. 2. 368)

In their spare turns, these lines almost depict the physical motions of grief and loss, and their unpretentious eloquence is a reflection of the peculiar force of Imogen's chaste energy

throughout the play. She is not Desdemona: her "tune" (V. 5.
238), to use Cymbeline's word for it, is different. She has, in
fact, much of Helena's purposiveness, and there is a vein of
asperity in her speech, reminiscent perhaps of Beatrice. Nevertheless, the image of her that abides is, like Desdemona's, that
of a woman so palpably and completely defined by the psychic
and spiritual experience of marriage that separation from her
husband is tantamount to separation from her self. Both senses
of separation are literalized in her disguise as Fidele.

Posthumus, correspondingly, has deep resemblances to
Othello. His gulling by Iachimo is a miniature of the great temptation scene of Iachimo's namesake Iago, and his behavior during the gulling suggests that though the wager may be conventional, his own part in it is not.[1] His praise of Imogen is too
showy and hyperbolic, he is too quick to barter her chastity –
Philario's dismay seems appropriate – and he is unquestionably
too quick to accept Iachimo's false report. As Philario again witnesses, he capitulates much before he has to or should. Like
Claudio as well as Othello, he believes the slander because he is
unconsciously disposed to do so, and as in the case of both
earlier characters his feverish fantasies of his wife's infidelities
are reflections of his own deep ambivalence towards her, of the
dissociation of feelings that causes him at once to over-idealize
her chastity and to resent and doubt it.

> Is there no way for men to be, but women
> Must be half-workers? We are all bastards,
> And that most venerable man which I
> Did call my father was I know not where
> When I was stamp'd. Some coiner with his tools
> Made me a counterfeit; yet my mother seem'd
> The Dian of that time. So doth my wife
> The nonpareil of this. O, vengeance, vengeance!
> Me of my lawful pleasure she restrain'd,
> And pray'd me oft forbearance; did it with
> A pudency so rosy, the sweet view on't
> Might well have warm'd old Saturn; that I thought her
> As chaste as unsunn'd snow. O, all the devils!
> This yellow Iachimo in an hour – was't not?

Or less! – at first? Perchance he spoke not, but,
Like a full-acorn'd boar, a German one,
Cried 'O!' and mounted; found no opposition
But what he look'd for should oppose and she
Should from encounter guard. Could I find out
The woman's part in me! For there's no motion
That tends to vice in man but I affirm
It is the woman's part.

(II. 5. 1)

A number of details in this speech resemble Claudio's accusations against Hero in the church scene in *Much Ado,* and though
its rather declamatory hysteria, which is accentuated in subsequent lines ("I'll write against them"), saves it from the seriousness of the comparable fantasies of Othello, Posthumus's
thoughts and associations, like Claudio's and more explicitly
than his, have ultimately the same roots as Othello's. His description of Imogen's restraint can have misleading modern
connotations but, as in Othello's fantasies about Desdemona's
cold chastity, the accent is upon Posthumus's distempered sexual appetite, not hers. His response to her chastity is clearly
tangled, and he himself suggests the configuration of Oedipal
guilt when he invokes the sexual relationship of his own parents, explicitly putting himself in the place of his father and
comparing Imogen to his mother. The anxiety of this fantasy is
amplified by our knowledge that Posthumus was orphaned at
birth.

If the characterizations of both Posthumus and Imogen are
reminiscent of *Othello,* however, many of the implications of
their erotic predicament are developed in ways more suggestive
of the problem comedies. To begin with, erotic disorder is associated with disorder in the kingdom. The separation of Posthumus and Imogen is continuously juxtaposed with the war
between Britain and Rome and the loss of Cymbeline's sons; and
the reunion of Posthumus and Imogen and the reconstitution of
their marriage is coextensive with the reunion of Cymbeline's
whole family and with the peace and union between Britain and
Rome. As in the problem comedies also, the root of the erotic

difficulties can be traced to the aggression and narcissism of
sensual appetite, a motif developed intensively in *Cymbeline*, as
we shall see, in the characterization of Cloten. As in *All's Well*,
that motif involves and provokes a conflict between the old and
the young, and as in *Measure for Measure* it leads, eventually, to a
confrontation with the fact of death. The famous song that
Guiderius sings over the body of Imogen is a lyric counterpart of
the Duke's meditative homily to Claudio. Imogen "dies" before
our eyes, and though we know she will revive (just as we know
that Claudio will not be executed), we respond to her sleep as
her brothers do, as an occasion for the acknowledgment of not
only the pain and loss of death, but its instinctual purpose and
consolation

> Fear no more the heat o' th' sun
>    Nor the furious winter's rages;
> Thou thy worldly task hast done,
>    Home art gone, and ta'en thy wages
> Golden lads and girls all must,
> As chimney-sweepers, come to dust.

(IV. 2. 259)

Posthumus experiences similar feelings when he welcomes
the prospect of his own death in the last act of the play and
when, in yet another analogue to the problem comedies, the
apprehension of death leads him to conceive of life in terms of
the parable of the talents:

> For Imogen's dear life take mine; and though
> 'Tis not so dear, yet 'tis a life; you coin'd it.
> 'Tween man and man they weigh not every stamp;
> Though light, take pieces for the figure's sake;
> You rather mine, being yours. And so, great pow'rs,
> If you will take this audit, take this life,
> And cancel these cold bonds. O Imogen!
> I'll speak to thee in silence. [*Sleeps.*]

(V. 4. 22)

The emphasis in this speech is Posthumus's own, but it also
grows out of the suggestiveness of the parable of the talents in
the whole matrix of the erotic action. Earlier in the play, during

his temptation of Posthumus, Iachimo turns the conventional financial images of a wager toward the consideration of Imogen's figurative preciousness ("she your jewel, this your jewel"), and during his temptation of Imogen herself, he insinuates, what is unfortunately to prove true, that "heaven's bounty towards" Posthumus might "Be us'd more thankfully. In himself, 'tis much; / In you, which I account his, beyond all talents" (I. 6. 77). As in both *Measure for Measure* and *All's Well*, the proper use of the talent of the heroine's chastity eventually enables the hero to make both psychic and spiritual profit of his erotic energy, and the heroine's integrity is represented as an animating and redemptive erotic force for the community as well as him. Imogen is particularly close to Helena in this respect, because as in *All's Well* her quest for reunion with her husband is the unifying impulse of the whole action, tying all the plots together, and her chastity, like Helena's, is actively associated with both supernatural and natural creative energies.

At the same time that *Cymbeline* draws upon the deeper motifs of both the problem comedies and *Othello*, however, its actual plot and the shape of its erotic action most closely resemble those of *Much Ado About Nothing*. Imogen's experience is fundamentally like Hero's, though it is more elaborated and less passive. At his first sight of Imogen, Iachimo says:

> All of her that is out of door most rich!
> If she be furnish'd with a mind so rare,
> She is alone th' Arabian bird, and I
> Have lost the wager.
>
> (I. 6. 15)

The number of physical disguises in *Cymbeline* is remarkable, and as in *Much Ado About Nothing* the disparity between the outer and inner person is a fundamental preoccupation of the play. Imogen, as Iachimo senses, is the miraculous bridge between the two. She is "faithful," even in disguise, and her chastity, like Hero's, provides an image and model of integrity in a world "o'ercome" with the "show" of the senses (V. 5. 54). Equally important, the Phoenix, the Arabian bird that died and

was reborn in its own ashes, was a traditional symbol of Christ,
and Iachimo's allusion to it in describing Imogen is especially
compelling because she literally enacts its significance. In *Much
Ado* the Friar looks "for greater birth" in Hero's feigned death,
and in the final scene both Hero and her father underline the
spiritual significance of her revival: "One Hero died defil'd; but I
do live, / And, surely as I live, I am a maid .. She died, my lord,
but whiles her slander liv'd" (V. 4. 63). As we have seen, however, Hero's "travail" has little direct impact upon Claudio and
even less on us, and the play's drama of regeneration is expressed in the characterizations of Dogberry and Beatrice and
Benedick. Hero's death and rebirth is schematically essential,
but it is largely figurative. In *Cymbeline* the figure is transformed
into literal action, and we actually experience the process by
which Imogen dies, "to be more fresh, reviving" (I 5. 42).

Similarly, Posthumus enacts a process of regeneration that is
only latent in the characterization of Claudio. In *Much Ado* the
Friar predicts, in language nourished by the deepest concerns of
the play, that the news of Hero's death will transform Claudio:

> When he shall hear she died upon his words,
> Th' idea of her life shall sweetly creep
> Into his study of imagination,
> And every lovely organ of her life
> Shall come apparell'd in more precious habit,
> More moving, delicate, and full of life,
> Into the eye and prospect of his soul,
> Than when she liv'd indeed.

(IV. 1. 223)

But this change in Claudio must largely be inferred. He reacts
callously to Hero's apparent death, and he repents. rather perfunctorily, only after he learns that she was innocent. Posthumus, however, truly undergoes the metamorphosis that the
Friar had planned for Claudio when, at the beginning of Act V,
Imogen indeed comes "into the eye and prospect" of his "soul,"
and he repents and forgives her before he learns that she is in
fact innocent The speech (V. 1. 1–33), which we shall examine
later in detail. follows closely upon Imogen's death and rebirth,

and it signals the beginning of the regenerative movement in the kingdom as well as within Posthumus.

There are intimations in the problem comedies of similar regenerative changes. Helena refers to the time in summer "When briers shall have leaves as well as thorns / And be as sweet as sharp" (IV. 4. 32), and, like Hero, she herself is reborn after she has been reported dead. In *Measure for Measure* Angelo and Claudio endure a penance not unlike Posthumus's, and the whole play suggests a sense of sexual charity comparable to that underlying Posthumus's forgiveness of Imogen. But these suggestions of the process of change, though important, are partial and circumscribed. The representation of regeneration in *Cymbeline* is not only more full, but different in kind. The problem comedies are to a large extent suspended between the characteristic experiences of *Othello* and *Much Ado About Nothing*: they draw upon the antinomies of tragedy and comedy without altering their separate natures. The lord's remark in *All's Well* that "The web of our life is of a mingled yarn, good and ill together" (IV. 3. 67), describes the generic tenor of the plays exactly. The erotic experience they depict is informed by the prospect of future growth, but good and ill, sweet and sharp, remain separable and distinct. In *Cymbeline*, on the other hand, these antinomies are not so much combined as dissolved, and the future prospect is fulfilled. The play moves *from* tragedy *to* comedy, from *Othello* to *Much Ado*, and it represents the process by which one is transformed into the other. This process of transformation, which is psychic as well as spiritual, is the fundamental subject of *Cymbeline*, as of all the final romances, and it suggests why the formal analogues that can make the play most intelligible are the mystery drama and dreams, both of them forms that represent elemental processes of transformation as well as a continuum of tragic and comic experience. The immanence of both these forms in *Cymbeline* is itself a function of what Frye has called the "deliberate archaism" of the last plays, their conscious regression to the primitive cadences of romance.

The congruence of a sacred and a primal drama is quite explicit in *Cymbeline*. Jupiter appears to Posthumus in a dream, and both Imogen and Posthumus call attention to the dreamlike nature of their experience at moments of great spiritual intensity. Imogen, just after her resurrection from sleep and her discovery of Cloten's headless body, says:

> Our very eyes
> Are sometimes, like our judgments, blind . . .
> The dream's here still. Even when I wake it is
> Without me, as within me; not imagin'd, felt.
>
> (IV. 2. 302)

Posthumus communicates a similar sensation following his repentance and his actual dream of a theophany:

> 'Tis still a dream, or else such stuff as madmen
> Tongue, and brain not; either both or nothing,
> Or senseless speaking, or a speaking such
> As sense cannot untie. Be what it is,
> The action of my life is like it, which
> I'll keep, if but for sympathy.
>
> (V. 4. 144)

These statements have an uncommon force in *Cymbeline*. They are not simply metaphors, but experiences that are related, in some ways more precisely and compellingly than in any other Shakespearean play, to the actual processes of dreaming.[2] These processes, and particularly those involving condensation and displacement, the two most fundamental mechanisms of dream-work, are endemic in the play, but they are especially pronounced in Shakespeare's representation of Posthumus and his relation to Cloten. Posthumus and Cloten are immediately paired at the opening of the play:

> He that hath miss'd the Princess is a thing
> Too bad for bad report; and he that hath her –
> I mean that married her, alack, good man!
> And therefore banish'd – is a creature such
> As, to seek through the regions of the earth
> For one his like, there would be something failing
> In him that should compare. I do not think

> So fair an outward and such stuff within
> Endows a man but he.
>
> (I. 1. 16)

This short-lived image of Posthumus predicates its opposite, and as the action progresses, the stuff within Posthumus does indeed so belie his outward appearance that Cloten begins to seem like his double.[3] Their minds become increasingly alike, Posthumus debasing Imogen in savagely jealous fantasies as Cloten does more directly in fantasies of rape, and eventually, in a sequence that culminates in the scene in which Imogen awakens beside Cloten's headless body, they look alike.

That sequence begins when Imogen, provoked beyond her endurance by Cloten's profane suit, tells him that he is too base to be Posthumus's groom and that Posthumus's

> mean'st garment
> That ever hath but clipp'd his body is dearer
> In my respect than all the hairs above thee,
> Were they all made such men.
>
> (II. 3. 133)

Cloten has hitherto been impervious to insults, but his own Parolles-like belief that the soul of a man is his clothes compels him to absorb this one. He repeats the phrase "mean'st garment" to himself no less than four times and leaves the stage with thoughts of revenge. Immediately following is the scene in which Posthumus accepts Iachimo's story, becomes obsessed with Cloten-like thoughts, and sends his vengeful and murderous letter to Pisanio. It is after Imogen reads this letter and must take flight in disguise, comfortless because she is now "Dead to [her] husband" (III. 4. 129), that Cloten significantly announces, "I love and hate her" (III. 5. 71), and makes his plans to ravish her wearing "the very garment of Posthumus" (III. 5. 136–7) to which she had compared him. He next appears on stage, in Posthumus's clothes, fully his surrogate in body if not in spirit:

> I am near to th' place where they should meet, if Pisanio have mapp'd it truly. How fit his garments serve me! Why should his

mistress, who was made by him that made the tailor, not be fit too? The rather – saving reverence of the word – for 'tis said a woman's fitness comes by fits. Therein I must play the workman. I dare speak it to myself, for it is not vain-glory for a man and his glass to confer in his own chamber – I mean, the lines of my body are as well drawn as his; no less young, more strong, not beneath him in fortunes, beyond him in the advantage of the time, above him in birth, alike conversant in general services, and more remarkable in single oppositions.

(IV. 1. 1)

Despite Cloten's half-comical grotesqueness, there is a truth to these lines upon which Shakespeare insists, for the physical resemblance between the two men is made painfully apparent by Imogen herself when she awakens to find Cloten beside her. Seeing the clothed but headless body, she mistakes it for her husband's:

> A headless man? The garments of Posthumus?
> I know the shape of's leg; this is his hand,
> His foot Mercurial, his Martial thigh,
> The brawns of Hercules; but his Jovial face–
> Murder in heaven!

(IV. 2. 309)

These lines have an oddly inhibiting artifice to which we shall return, but for the moment we should also note the seriousness both of Imogen's speech and her predicament. Posthumus himself has been entirely absent from the stage for nearly two acts when she makes this speech, but throughout that time, Cloten, dressed in his clothes, has presented us with an undeniable image of him. Imogen's grief, therefore, though misplaced, is not only real but appropriate, because for us as well as her, Posthumus has in fact become psychically and spiritually merged with the headless corpse that lies beside her.

Among the deepest of the buried metaphors of *Much Ado About Nothing* is sexual fashion, Borachio's apparel of concupiscence. In *All's Well* Parolles wears that apparel on stage, and in *Cymbeline* the metaphor is once again brought on stage as Posthumus's "mean'st garment" and is given a literal life (and death). The garment itself, with its condensed visual and verbal impact, makes clear, I think, that Cloten and Posthumus are disunited parts of a single psychic entity and that Cloten is in essence a manifestation of Posthumus's unconscious, an expression of the primitive feelings of sensual aggression toward Imogen that Posthumus cannot accept in his conscious thought but that profoundly decompose and polarize his love for her. The conflict is partially depicted in his murderous jealousy itself, a jealousy identical in kind to Othello's; but its fullest and starkest consequences are represented in Cloten, and more than any other single element, this displacement gives the play the configuration of a dream and accounts for its capacity to amalgamate the erotic experience of *Othello* and *Much Ado About Nothing,* as well as that of the problem comedies. The emotional destructiveness of sexual polarization, which is internalized and made tragically inescapable in *Othello* and only partially allayed in the other plays, is both fully represented and ultimately resolved in its transposition to Cloten. It is Cloten who literally decomposes, and it is he who acts out the buried antinomies of erotic life.

The statement, "I love and hate her," is an explicit enough indication of the tenor of Cloten's characterization, but the aggression he represents is most resonant in the scene in which he woos Imogen with his famous aubade, "Hark, hark! the lark."

> I would this music would come. I am advised to give her music a mornings; they say it will penetrate.
>
> *Enter* MUSICIANS.
>
> Come on, tune. If you can penetrate her with your fingering, so. We'll try with tongue too. If none will do, let her remain; but I'll never give o'er. First, a very excellent good-conceited thing; after a wonderful sweet air, with admirable rich words to it – and then let her consider.
>
> *Song.*
>
>> Hark, hark! the lark at heaven's gate sings,
>>     And Phoebus 'gins arise,
>> His steeds to water at those springs

On chalic'd flow'rs that lies;
And winking Mary-buds begin
To ope their golden eyes.
With everything that pretty bin,
My lady sweet, arise;
Arise, arise!

So get you gone. If this penetrate, I will consider your music
the better; if it do not, it is a vice in her ears which horsehairs
and calves' guts, nor the voice of unpaved eunuch to boot, can
never amend.

(II. 3. 11)

The contrast between profane and sacred love could not be more
apparent, and it is expanded and intensified by the full context
of the action, for immediately prior to this song Iachimo views
the sleeping Imogen and calls attention to another bird and
another pole of erotic experience:

She hath been reading late
The tale of Tereus; here the leaf's turn'd down
Where Philomel gave up.... I lodge in fear;
Though his a heavenly angel, hell is here.

(II. 2. 44)

The music of the lark and the rape of Philomel are explicitly
contrasted in a song in Lyly's *Campaspe* that Shakespeare may
have expected his audience to know,[4] but in any case Shakespeare conveys the spiritual and psychological implications of the
contrast directly enough, and with great power, in the juxtaposition of the two scenes. The sight of Iachimo voyeuristically
violating Imogen, the loveliness of the music of the aubade as
well as the beauty of its language, and the brutishness of Cloten's single-minded phallic aggression are representations of a
radical polarization of erotic feeling, and the whole sequence is a
proleptic image of the psychic drama that transpires in Posthumus's jealousy.

The resolution of that drama depends, of course, upon the
death of Cloten and of the unconscious aggression and guilt
within Posthumus that Cloten's merger with his garment has
symbolized. As we have seen, this figurative death becomes an

emotional fact of Imogen's experience when she grieves for Posthumus, while at the same time her own reawakening from "death" prepares us for his renewed love for her and for his rebirth as the regenerated figure who appears at the beginning of Act V, and whose very first words after his long absence from the stage are of sexual forgiveness:

> Yea, bloody cloth, I'll keep thee; for I wish'd
> Thou shouldst be colour'd thus. You married ones,
> If each of you should take this course, how many
> Must murder wives much better than themselves
> For wrying but a little!
>
> (V. 1. 1)

These lines suggest a transformation even more radical than that which the Friar predicts for Claudio in *Much Ado About Nothing*, for Posthumus forgives Imogen not only without knowing, but without even feeling, that she is innocent of adultery. The lines are a caution not to confuse Shakespeare's emphasis upon chastity with moralistic repressiveness, Christian or otherwise. Posthumus's words suggest the obvious general truth that adultery is hardly to be compared with man's more destructive impulses, but even more important is their erotic charity. His forgiveness of Imogen is reminiscent of the sexual experience that Shakespeare adduces in *Measure for Measure* from the scriptural text, "Judge not, that ye be not judged," but it goes far deeper, not only because it explicitly comprehends adultery, as the earlier play does not, but because, through Posthumus's whole relation to Cloten, Shakespeare actually represents the unconscious erotic process that is the source of his forgiveness.

Far more directly than the action of *All's Well*, the entire drama of Posthumus's psyche that is played out in Cloten's pursuit of Imogen has evocations of the fable of Beauty and the Beast, and, as in the fable as well as the earlier play, it is only when the beast is assimilated that it can be exorcised and that love can flourish and the Prince come back to life. The displacement of Posthumus's beastliness onto Cloten permits his repressed sexual aggression to be actively expressed and incorporated into a comic resolution rather than simply denied or purged; and it enables Shakespeare to represent a fully articulated dramatic resolution to the profound problem of erotic guilt that is adumbrated in the earlier comedies and that constitutes the heart of Othello's tragedy. Posthumus is cured of the same jealousy that afflicts Othello because the unconscious connection between repressed aggression and guilt is broken. The beast that is part of Posthumus's unconscious life, as of the life of all men, finds both expression and release. Cloten is literally beheaded, which in dreams usually signifies castration; but the deeper import of his representation in the play is the harmonious incorporation of much of his energy in the regenerated Posthumus. A precisely analogous expression and incorporation of aggression is enacted in the political plot of the play, as Britain first wars against (and actually defeats) Rome, before it willingly pays the tribute that brings the "harmony" of "peace" (V. 5. 465). All the final plays are concerned with a similar process, but none represents its erotic dynamics so fully and precisely as *Cymbeline*.

Posthumus himself, of course, is entirely unaware of Cloten's drama; he is literally unconscious of it. But we ourselves experience that drama, fully, and because we do, we are in a position to understand how, when Posthumus forgives Imogen's "wrying," he comes to terms, unconsciously as well as consciously, with not only her sexuality but his own. As he continues to talk of Imogen, he once again idealizes her as a gift of the gods – "Imogen is your own" (V. 1. 16) – but now without a trace of psychic conflict or guilt, and his erotic harmony and the renewal of his love immediately result in a visible transformation of his identity. He vows to change his clothes:

> I'll disrobe me
> Of these Italian weeds, and suit myself
> As does a British peasant. So I'll fight
> Against the part I come with; so I'll die
> For thee, O Imogen, even for whom my life
> Is every breath a death. And thus unknown,

> Pitied nor hated, to the face of peril
> Myself I'll dedicate. Let me make men know
> More valour in me than my habits show.
> Gods, put the strength o' th' Leonati in me!
> To shame the guise o' th' world, I will begin
> The fashion – less without and more within.
>
> (V. 1. 22)

This speech is the axis of the many revolutions that eventually result in the regeneration not only of Posthumus's family but of Cymbeline's and the kingdom's. It is therefore particularly important that the change it signifies is in the first instance individual and erotic: the resolution of the unconscious guilt that has alienated Posthumus from himself as well as his wife. This psychodrama is the core of all the other transformations in the play, political as well as individual, and it clearly expresses the sense, which is explicit in the liturgy of Matrimony, that the capacity to love another as one's self is the psychic and spiritual paradigm not only of an individual soul but of a community.

The spiritual implications of Posthumus's transformation are coordinate with the psychic ones and even more transparent. The whole process by which his marriage with Imogen is reconstituted suggests all the marvelously condensed meanings of the word "atone" in Hymen's description, in *As You Like It*, of the union of husband and wife:

> Then is there mirth in heaven,
> When earthly things made even
> Atone together.
>
> (V. 4. 102)

The Atonement itself is suggested most directly and richly in Imogen's sacrificial death and rebirth, but Posthumus's actions too eventually convey the sense of his reconciliation not only with himself but with God. His discussion and change of clothes, echoing Borachio's meditation on fashion, literalize the Pauline metaphor of spiritual regeneration, the putting off of "the olde man, which is corrupt through the deceivable lustes," and the putting on of "the new man, which after God is created in righteousness, and true holiness" (Eph. iv. 22, 24). Later, after the British victory, when he pretends to be a Roman and is taken prisoner, he makes a speech of repentance that precisely describes the stages necessary for the remission of sins[5] and that ends, in the passage I quoted earlier, with his offering his life for Imogen's as part of the final "audit" of his talents: "For Imogen's dear life take mine; and though / 'Tis not so dear, yet 'tis a life; you coin'd it" (V.4.22). Because we know that Imogen has died and been reborn for his sake, we know also, in the words of the Geneva gloss to the parable of the talents, that he will "continue in the knowledge of God, and do good with those graces yt God hathe given [him]." Posthumus's speech of repentance is immediately succeeded by the dream reaffirming his name and family, and like his change of clothes both the speech and the dream suggest the pattern of spiritual rebirth that is modelled after and made possible by Christ's sacrifice. I think they also have specific overtones of baptism, a sacrament that explicitly describes a process of death and rebirth and that verifies the identity of the individual by incorporating him into the larger family of God's "holy congregation" (Liturgy of Baptism, *Book of Common Prayer*). There is certainly a sense of Britain's baptism as a nation at the end of the play in its incorporation into Rome and into the peace that ushered in the birth of Christ.[6] A union with Rome is significantly opposed by Cloten, whose jingoism is the political equivalent, and expression, of Posthumus's psychic aggression and narcissism.

Northrop Frye has argued that Shakespeare may have chosen the historical milieu of *Cymbeline* in part because "Cymbeline was king of Britain at the time of Christ," and he suggests that "the sense of a large change in human fortunes taking place off-stage has to be read into *Cymbeline*," even though, "as a rule reading things into Shakespeare in the light of some external information is a dubious practice."[7] I think Frye is right, though it seems to me that the significance of the contemporaneous life of Christ is sufficiently inherent in the play not to require the kind of extrinsic reading to which he objects.[8] As I have suggested, the play has many Christian images that are precisely defined and have a manifest spiritual referent. Posthumus's penitential transformation is one example, but there are many others, and the entire action, and especially the erotic action, is governed by a redemptive and providential conception of experience. "Some griefs," Imogen says, "doth physic love" (III. 2. 33), and this idea in particular, the paradox of the fortunate fall, is pronounced in the play. The paradox is, of course, virtually a generic requirement of a comic action, and as we have seen it is present in abundance in *Much Ado* as well as the problem comedies. Its use in *Cymbeline*, however, is more self-conscious than in the earlier works, even than in *All's Well*, as if Shakespeare wished to call attention to the actual dynamics of the process of change that it signifies. The paradox is repeated in the action and language of the play over and over again, in the numerous enactments of death and rebirth, and in many speeches.It is insistently linked to the play's preoccupation with the disjunction between outer and inner life and it informs the whole pattern of experience not only of Imogen and Posthumus, but of the entire kingdom of Britain. We are made aware at the start of the play that the potion that the Queen gives Imogen is not only harmless, but beneficent:

> there is
> No danger in what show of death it makes,
> More than the locking up the spirits a time,
> To be more fresh, reviving.
>
> (I. 5. 39)

We ourselves witness the power of the paradox when we see Imogen dying to (and for) her old husband to be reborn to a new one, and Lucius makes the experience explicit when he tells her:

> Be cheerful; wipe thine eyes.
> Some falls are means the happier to arise.
>
> (IV. 2. 405)

Precisely the same idea is made explicit in the characterization of Posthumus at the end of the play as he himself senses the death of his old self and as Jupiter appears in his dream with the explanation that makes his suffering intelligible.

Whom best I love I cross; to make my gift,
The more delay'd, delighted. Be content;
Your low-laid son our godhead will uplift;
His comforts thrive, his trials well are spent.
Our Jovial star reign'd at his birth, and in
Our temple was he married. Rise, and fade!
He shall be lord of Lady Imogen,
And happier much by his affliction made.

(V. 4. 101)

Jupiter's appearance makes manifest the providential power that has been immanent in the play from the start, and as with the comparable scenes in Shakespeare's other romances it suggests the theophanies of the mystery drama. The birth of Christ in the Nativity plays is at once the cause and result of the charity that transforms the shepherds' lives, just as the vision of Jupiter is simultaneously the divine origin and concrete manifestation of the spiritual transformation of Posthumus and Britain. The sense, therefore, of a transcendent change in human fortune in *Cymbeline*, though it ultimately has an offstage Christ as its referent, is also inherent in the very structure of the play, for like biblical history in the mystery drama, Shakespeare's legendary history of the nativity of Britain is essentially a spiritual fable, the revelation in time of a reality that exists outside of it.

That transcendent reality, as I have been emphasizing, is also a psychic one in the play, and it is of great significance that Jupiter should appear to Posthumus in a dream, the form of psychic experience that itself suggests analogies with the mystery drama. Freud called dreams "*the royal road to a knowledge of the unconscious activities of the mind*,"[9] and there are a number of ideas in his interpretation of dreams, beyond those that I have been suggesting, that illuminate the peculiar capacity of *Cymbeline* to represent a confluence of psychic and spiritual experience. Three areas of Freud's thinking on dreams seem to me especially fertile in interpreting *Cymbeline*. as well as the last plays as a group. The first concerns the dream-wish. The dream-wish is not, as it is often construed, the proclamation of a happy ending, but a structural principle. Freud argued that at the heart of a dream is an unconscious impulse seeking and finding satisfaction:

> For there is no doubt about it: this unconscious impulse is the true creator of the dream; it is what produces the psychical energy for the dream's construction. Like any other instinctual impulse, it cannot strive for anything other than its own satisfaction; and our experience in interpreting dreams shows us too that that is the sense of all dreaming. In every dream an instinctual wish has to be represented as fulfilled.[10]

The fulfillment of the wish, however, takes work, and it is that work that constitutes the characteristic texture and experience of dreaming. Freud argued that though resistance to unconscious impulses is markedly reduced in sleep, these impulses are still subject to censorship, and the dream as a result is not only born of conflict but represents it. Most dreams consist both of manifest thoughts, often the residue of waking thoughts, which are admissible to consciousness, and latent thoughts, which are unconscious and usually repressed, but which in the dream find expression through indirect and circuitous mechanisms of transformation such as displacement and condensation. Animating these latent thoughts is the unconscious impulse that constitutes the dream-wish. The dream-wish, therefore, defines not only the dream's goal, but the process that allows the goal to be realized. This deep process, a rich and varied movement of primitive psychic forces, which is finally a compromise between the dreamer's conscious and unconscious life, Freud called dream-work, and it makes up the actual experience of the dream.[11]

The manifest dream-wish of Posthumus's dream as well as of the whole erotic action of *Cymbeline* is that Posthumus should be reunited with his wife, that he should "be lord of Lady Imogen / And happier much by his affliction made." The reason, however, that we ourselves can find that outcome satisfying is that we have witnessed the dream-work that composes it, for behind the rebirth of Posthumus's love for Imogen lies a profound psychic experience of precisely the erotic forces that most threaten it. Posthumus's sexual guilt, the impulse in his love for Imogen of which his jealousy is finally only a symptom, the sexual aggression and narcissism that are constituents of all erotic love but that are also related to rape, and more mysteriously, to death – these unconscious drives within Posthumus are worked through, as we have seen, as they would be in a dream, by displacement onto the figures of Cloten, and less obviously, Imogen herself. The displacement, of course, is not part either of Posthumus' actual dream or of his consciousness, which may account for an impression of diffuseness in the play, because the psychic experience of the hero in the other romances is more fully interrealized and therefore seems more natural, more proximate to the articulations of waking life We find the literally pathological decomposition of Leontes in *The Winter's Tale*, for example, more credible, if not necessarily more comprehensible. But if that displacement in *Cymbeline* is not a part of Posthumus's direct experience, it is unmistakably a part of ours. It governs our response to him and to all the changes in the play of which his is the paradigm, and it confirms the truth of his regeneration to our own experience. The idea of *felix culpa*, of being made eventually happier by affliction, is of all Christian premises the most uncomfortable to modern sensibility, but we should recognize not only that it can in fact occur in our waking life, though not as often as we might wish, but that it constitutes the fundamental process of our dreams, the psychic experience we all share, in which suffering is habitually transformed into satisfaction and "tragedy" is regularly incorporated into "comedy." The pattern of tragicomedy is the pattern of our dreams, and though the triumph of the pleasure principle is in both cases fictive – hallucinatory in the dream, and illusory in the play – it is a fiction that draws upon a profound reality of psychic life. The critics who have been inclined to attribute the depiction of pain and suffering in the problem plays as well as the romances to covert cynicism or artistic weariness thus quite miss the point. [12] The representation of suffering in these plays is the sign of deep comic work and hope, particularly in the romances, where the very cadence of suffering is transformation. Ariel uses the word "suffer" itself in exactly this sense in the song that lies at the heart of *The Tempest:*

> Nothing of him that doth fade
> But doth suffer a sea-change
> Into something rich and strange.

> (I. 2. 399)

The unconscious is the source of hope, as it is of the dream-wish, and because the unconscious is the home of the indestructible, eternal, impulses of our childhood, the dream-wish is always a recapitulation of the past. This is the second feature of dreams that I think is relevant to an understanding of *Cymbeline*, and in this case to Posthumus's actual dream. At the close of *The Interpretation of Dreams* Freud wrote:

> And the value of dreams for giving us knowledge of the future? There is of course no question of that. It would be truer to say instead that they give us knowledge of the past. For dreams are derived from the past in every sense. Nevertheless the ancient belief that dreams foretell the future is not wholly devoid of truth. By picturing our wishes as fulfilled, dreams are after all leading us into the future. But this future, which the dreamer pictures as the present, has been moulded by his indestructible wish into a perfect likeness of the past. [13]

It seems to me that this description is almost an exact psychological equivalent of the Christian conception of providential time that we find enacted in the mystery drama. It is certainly a perfect likeness of the action of *The Second Shepherds' Play*, in which the wish for charity leads the shepherds to travel backwards in time to discover the Nativity that is eternally present in their lives. In the Renaissance, a similar conception of time is stated in lines like the following from Spenser's "Mutability Cantos":

> All things stedfastnes do hate
> And changed be: yet being rightly wayd
> They are not changed from their first estate;

But by their change their being co dilate:
And turning to themselves at length againe,
Doe worke their own perfection so by fate.[14]

Spenser's passage has often been used by critics as a gloss to explain "th' argument of Time" (*Winter's Tae*, IV. 1. 29) and of providential immanence we experience in the last plays; and its resemblance to Freud's anatomy of the sense of time in a dream is remarkable.

In any case, however, both a religious and psychological apprehension of an eternal present are almost schematically explicit in Posthumus's dream – the religious manifestation, as we have seen, in the theophany of Jupiter, and its psychic analogue in the actual construction of the cream. For though Jupiter directly predicts the future, the primary experience of the dream – for Posthumus – is a return to the estate of childhood. Posthumus himself does not appear in the dream; the ghosts of his family recount his sufferings, and Jupiter addresses them. Posthumus had earlier speculated on his parentage, in particular the fidelity of his mother, and as his name emphasizes he is an orphan, separated at birth from his family In the dream it is the recovery of his loving brothers and parents, the recovery of a childhood literally lost, that enables him to reintegrate himself as a man and reunite with Imogen, just as Britain can reconstitute itself and look to a future union with Rome only when it recovers its own lost children. Posthumus's vision of his family may not be as moving as the comparable scenes in the last acts of *Pericles, The Winter's Tale*, and *Cymbeline*, where the process by which a man is remade by a return to childhood is acted out in a literal reunion with his own child, but it is psychologically of a piece with those reunions and it reflects the general disposition of the final plays to present condensed images of the cycles of nature and of human history as well as of individual human life.

The final analogy between *Cymbeline* and dream-work is revealed in the play's unusual tone. That tone has given many critics the impression that Shakespeare "is somehow *playing* with the play,"[15] and it disconcerts them. Dr. Johnson's exasperation, once again, is typical:

This play has many just sentiments, some natural dialogues, and some pleasing scenes, but they are obtained at the expence of much incongruity.
    To remark the folly of the fiction, the absurdity of the conduct, the confusion of names and manners of different times, and the impossibility of the events in any system of life, were to waste criticism upon unresisting imbecillity, upon faults too evident for detection, and too gross for aggravation.[16]

The extreme heterogeneity of action, time and place upon which Johnson remarks is, of course, a primary characteristic of dream experience, and he is right in seeing it in *Cymbeline*, even though he is unsympathetic to it. There is a strong sense of incongruity, as well as of detachment, in *Cymbeline's* action and style, and such incongruity can be puzzling because it seems to mute our responses and prevent us from knowing what should or should not be taken seriously. The conjunction, in particular, of a sense of detachment with odd and powerful pulses of feeling is common in the play and is especially acute in the depiction of Imogen and of the events surrounding her. I have focused mainly upon Posthumus in discussing the anatomy of psychic and spiritual change in the play, but it is Imogen whose radiant constancy and love generate both his and the kingdom's transformation; it is she whose pilgrimage gathers up all the filaments of the action; and it is preeminently she to whom everything at once most disturbing and outrageous happens in the play. As we have seen, she herself describes the pressure of the action surrounding her as a dream, and the whole of that speech, which occurs at a highly charged moment of the action, after she has just awakened from her own burial and discovered the headless body of Cloten, is revealing:

> These flow'rs are like the pleasures of the world;
> This bloody man, the care on't. I hope I dream;
> For so I thought I was a cave-keeper,
> And cook to honest creatures. But 'tis not so;

'Twas but a bolt of nothing, shot at nothing,
Which the brain makes of fumes. Our very eyes
Are sometimes, like our judgments, blind. Good faith,
I tremble still with fear; but if there be
Yet left in heaven as small a drop of pity
As a wren's eye, fear'd gods, a part of it!
The dreams's here still. Even when I wake it is
Without me, as within me; not imagin'd, felt.
A headless man? The garments of Posthumus?
I know the shape of's leg; this is his hand.
His foot Mercurial, his Martial thigh,
The brawns of Hercules; but his Jovial face –
Murder in heaven!

(IV. 2. 297)

This speech and its context, which are typical of the whole action of *Cymbeline*, has troubled critics greatly. Even Granville-Barker, who had considerable sympathy with the play, protested that

It is a fraud on Imogen; and we are accomplices in it. We have watched the playwright's plotting, been amused by his ingenuity. We shall even be a little conscious as we watch, in this sophisticated play, of the big bravura chance given to the actress. But Imogen herself is put, quite needlessly, quite heartlessly, on exhibition. How shall we sympathize with such futile suffering? And surely it is a faulty art that can so make sport of its creatures.[17]

As Granville-Barker himself partially perceived, however, suffering has its own peculiar cadence in this play, and the scene's art, which is in any case more effective on stage than it might appear to be on paper, is also more intelligible when it is understood in terms of dream experience. Freud remarked that a dream most insists on the "right to be included among our real mental experiences" on the basis of its "affects," its feelings. He pointed out, however, that these feelings are frequently quite disproportionate to the "ideational" content of the dream and that when "the affect and the idea are incompatible in their character and intensity, our waking judgment is at a loss." The problem disappears, he argued, when we move from the manifest to latent content of the dream, for the affects are the unaltered expression of the dream's deepest thoughts, and where they seem incompatible with the manifest content, it is the ideational material that "*has undergone displacement and substitutions.*"[18] As we have seen, such displacements and substitutions are essentially elaborate artifices, disguises over which the dreamer can exert some conscious control. At the same time, because their purpose is to release latent dream thoughts of tremendous emotional power, their final effect is paradoxical. They may partially drain actors and actions in the dream of the affect that would be appropriate to them in waking life, but that affect is by no means lost. It animates the mechanisms of dream-work in the first place and it is expressed in the dream-wish that lies at the heart of the dream. The very nature of a dream, therefore, leads it to develop a style like that of Imogen's speech, a style that combines a high degree of control and artfulness with a suffusion of primitive and powerful feeling.

This combination also marks the style of *Cymbeline* as a whole. Like all the romances, the play deliberately places us at some distance from its action and heightens our awareness of its language and theatrical contrivance. Granville-Barker himself shrewdly suggested that Shakespeare

has an unlikely story to tell, and in its unlikelihood lies not only its charm, but largely its very being; reduce it to reason, you would wreck it altogether. Now in the theater there are two ways of dealing with the inexplicable. If the audience are to take it seriously, leave it unexplained. They will be anxious – pathetically anxious – to believe you; with faith in the dose, they will swallow a lot. The other plan is to show one's hand, saying in effect: 'Ladies and gentlemen, this is an exhibition of tricks, and what I want you to enjoy among other things is the skill with which I hope to perform them.' This art, which deliberately displays its art, is very suited to a tragi-comedy, to the telling of a serious story that must yet not be taken too seriously, lest its comedy be swamped by its tragedy and a happy ending become too incongruous.[19]

I think Granville-Barker is right, although because he does not appreciate the unconscious and transcendental ligaments between the tragedy and the happy ending, he places too much emphasis upon the play's showmanship and not enough on its capacity to move us. He perceives the character of the play's affects, but not their intensity.

He comes closer to such a perception in his discussion of the play's verse. Shakespeare, he remarks,

seems to be cultivating a new Euphuism. It has no close likeness to the old; by the difference, indeed, we may measure something of the distance he has traveled in twenty years of playwrighting. It is a Euphuism of imagination rather than expression. This will often be simple enough; it is the thought or emotion behind that may seem far-fetched for the occasion or the speaker.[20]

As I have argued elsewhere, Shakespeare's company had just acquired the Blackfriars theater at the time he was writing *Cymbeline,* and he may have been stimulated to develop this kind of style by the self-conscious declamations of the coterie plays of Marston and Fletcher.[21] But the sense of "a Euphuism of the imagination," of an incongruous charge of thought and feeling behind the verse and the occasion, is peculiar to *Cymbeline* and the last plays and is a clear analogue of the condensed and displaced energies of expression in dreams.

The "exhibition" of Imogen's grief over the headless body of Cloten has just such an expressive energy behind its coterie facade. The scene italicizes its own contrivance and compels us to attend to it as a theatrical fiction: we know that the headless figure is not Posthumus's; the body itself has become virtually a stage prop, cauterized by the vaguely comic artifice that has marked Cloten's characterization from the start of the play and that is particularly evident in the scene that leads to his decapitation; and Imogen's classical allusions have a tincture of a similar comic anaesthesia. At the same time, however, these very artifices release the energies of the scene's deeper content, the profound process of erotic change within Posthumus, the character whose psyche and spirit truly are present in the body and garments over which Imogen grieves. It is to this content – in essence Posthumus's fortunate fall – that the complex affect of the scene belongs, and its peculiar style frees us to feel both Imogen's real pain and the promise of a deliverance of which she herself is yet unaware. This condensed combination of feelings and perceptions can perhaps best be described as wonder, and it is exactly true to the experience of rebirth and transformation that informs the idea of *felix culpa*. It is also true to the experience of dreams.

Shakespeare explicitly describes the nature of wonder in an apposite and rich passage in *The Winter's Tale* in which a courtier recounts the reunion of Leontes and Perdita:

> I make a broken delivery of the business; but the changes I perceived in the King and Camillo were very notes of admiration. They seem'd almost, with staring on one another, to tear the cases of their eyes; there was speech in their dumbness, language in their very gesture; they look'd as they had heard of a world ransom'd, or one destroyed. A notable passion of wonder appeared in them; but the wisest beholder that knew no more but seeing could not say if th' importance were joy or sorrow – but in the extremity of the one it must needs be.
>
> (V. 2. 9)

These metaphors describe an essential experience not only of *The Winter's Tale* but of all the final romances, and they are particularly close to the texture of *Cymbeline*. In *The Winter's Tale* itself, whose erotic plot is similar to *Cymbeline*'s, the extremities of sexual guilt and erotic rebirth are embodied in the whole diptych construction of the play, and the movement from one part to the other, the process by which Leontes's deathlike jealousy is healed and his family reborn, is represented in largely natural terms, through the growth of his child and the actual passage of time. Even the epiphany of Hermione's resurrection, in which the warmth of life truly does give speech to dumbness and language to gesture, is kept a surprise from us as well as Leontes, and remains rationally explicable. The statue itself has the wrinkles of age. In *Cymbeline* the same changes of wonder are represented, but they are less obedient to the laws of conscious experience. Time is simultaneously condensed and dilated, as it is both in the mystery drama and dreams, and the play returns us more directly, as those forms do, to the transcendental and primal processes of transformation. In *Cym-*

*beline,* as in the mystery drama, one world literally is ransomed and another destroyed, and the epiphany of that movement is confirmed in the actual manifestation of a god; and in the psychic drama of *Cymbeline* the resolution of erotic guilt is achieved through the "senseless speaking, or a speaking such / As sense cannot untie" of an actual dream within a play as well as through the style of dream-work in the whole of the drama. I think it is the return to these primal and sacred forms in *Cymbeline* that makes its theatrical self-consciousness seem finally so numinous and that enables the play as a whole to represent so great a range of erotic experience.

# 7

# Conclusion

The erotic plots of all the plays I have discussed in this study are drawn, at least in part, from Italian novelle. The novelle were a storehouse of such plots, but equally important, they provided the form in the later Middle Ages and the Renaissance that perhaps most encouraged an examination of the texture and particularity of relations among men and women. I think that some of the unusual domesticity of Shakespeare's plots and characterizations was developed from this tradition. Desdemona speaking of Othello putting on his gloves, and Imogen of lying awake at night thinking of Posthumous "twixt clock and clock," the tics of familiarity in Benedick's and Beatrice's encounters, the sense of Isabella's family relationship, as well as Bertram's both with his mother and Helena – these synapses of domestic intimacy and details of everyday life grow naturally out of the stories in the novelle and help account for Shakespeare's capacity to represent the manners of love (as well as of other human relationships) with such immediacy and fullness.

At the same time, however, one has only to read Cinthio, Bandello, or even Boccaccio, to realize how essentially different Shakespeare's plays are and how inappropriate it is to think of them primarily in terms of psychological or social realism. Much of the mischief in *Othello* criticism, for example, comes from the disposition to treat the play simply as a richer or better version of the kind of tale from which it is derived. But there is nothing either above or below the surface of the love story in Cinthio. The handkerchief is only a handkerchief, and Othello can be understood precisely and only as a gullible and jealous Moor. In

Shakespeare, on the other hand, the handkerchief is not only a token of Othello's love but a condensation of his whole psychic history, and the very features of his character that give him individual definition, his color and his age, simultaneously enlarge and generalize his condition. His character itself is intelligible less as a whole personality than as a condensation of elemental fragments, a shifting palimpsest of Desdemona's love and Iago's hate. The story of love in *Othello* is profoundly resonant. The surface retains a literal and important life, but it also expresses realms that transcend the palpable logic of the senses and that include the mysteries of faith and of the unconscious.

The same is true of the other plays we have discussed. The idea of the Hero and Claudio plot in *Much Ado About Nothing* is ancient and is found in Ariosto as well as Bandello, but in none of these sources, and certainly not in Bandello, is there comparable depth. The wedding ceremony that is aborted in the middle of *Much Ado* is not simply a melodramatic narrative episode, for the meaning of the ceremony radiates through the play; and the whole plot of Hero and Claudio, both in itself and in its continuous collocation with the wit of Benedick and Beatrice as well as the innocence of Dogberry, becomes an anatomy for the representation of the spiritual and psychic process by which men and women are joined in love.

The problem comedies are somewhat closer to their sources because Shakespeare is as interested as Cinthio and Boccaccio are in the mundane complications of the erotic plot and in the intellectual issues that they generate. But the very conception of erotic energy is different in Shakespeare. In Boccaccio the bedtrick is simply a trick, and although it is conveyed with a sophisticated sense of irony, there is no intimation of the kinds of paradoxes of the flesh and spirit that Helena experiences and reflects upon in *All's Well That Ends Well*, nor is there a comparable sense of Helena's creative as well as procreative vitality. Nor does Boccaccio place his erotic action, as Shakespeare does, within the whole continuum of human growth. Similarly, though the design of *Measure for Measure* can be found in

Cinthio, its essential experience cannot. There is no interest in Cinthio in the erotic composition of the characters who are the counterparts of Angelo, Isabella, and Claudio, and there is certainly nothing corresponding to Shakespeare's exploration of the dialectic of sexual repression and license or of the erotic dynamics of charity.

Finally, in *Cymbeline*, though the wager plot is indebted to Boccaccio, as in *Much Ado About Nothing* it is deepened by being continuously related to other plots in the play. The deception of Posthumus is the occasion for the virtual decomposition of his personality, and the resolution of his inner guilt and reconstitution of his love and marriage represent a paradigm of spiritual and psychic transformation. The whole play eventually defines erotic energy in the largest possible terms, as the source of both individual and social integrity.

I think that both Freudian psychology and Christian theology are relevant to the interpretation of these representations of erotic life, and as I have repeatedly argued the two are often more similar than might at first be supposed. My own justification for the value of making analogies between Freud and the Bible finally rests on the validity of the actual interpretations I have proposed, but it is worth recapitulating some of the fundamental analogies that I have been suggesting in this study. Freud himself would not have welcomed these comparisons and there are many writers who still find them offensive. Because, however, there are Freudian analysts who are believing Christians, just as there are Christian theologians committed to Freudian thought, the issue is not entirely a theoretical one. In any event, despite his attacks on religion, Freud's own way of thinking about human behavior as well as his own temperament in fact have much in common with St. Paul's. St. Paul, for example, acknowledges the presence of a force in his life superior to his conscious will, which he says "dwelleth in me" and which he calls "the law in my members," and he occasionally speaks of it directly in terms suggesting the unconscious: "For I alowe not that which I do: for what I wolde, that do I not: but what I hate, that do I" (Rom. vii, 20, 23, 15). Freud, fcr his part, postulates a myth of the primal horde that corresponds structurally in his thinking to the Fall in Christian thought, and though he hardly regarded the law in his members as sinful, his treatment of the Oedipal conflict as a source of inescapable sexual guilt in effect closely parallels the Pauline sense of original sin.[1] Freud's sexual pessimism is most pronounced in *Civilization and Its Discontents* (1930), but it is evident in "The Most Common Form of Degradation in Erotic Life" (1912), and it pervades his work.

There is, I think, a comparable similarity between Freudian and Christian ideas of primal innocence. Freud's references to paradise as a group fantasy of childhood are invidious, but he nevertheless also refers frequently, as the Bible does, to childhood as an idyllic model, and his conception of primary narcissism operates in his thinking much as the quest for a return to Eden does in Christian thought. Moreover, though he has no interest in an after-life, he is consistently concerned with the phylogenetic inheritances of human nature, and his conception of the id itself, if not of the entire realm of the unconscious, suggests fundamental analogies with Christian ideas of eternity and of heaven and hell. And as in the Christian epistemology of a parable like that of the talents, the unconscious, the true psychical reality, is conceived at once as something given, if not a gift, derived from outside the self, and as an inner resource.

Finally, most significant, and certainly most germane to this study, is the profound emphasis in both Freud and the Bible upon the mysteries and importance of love in forming both a whole individual and a whole community. Christian charity has an ultimately eschatological focus, but even in St. Paul, whose distaste for genital sexuality is pronounced, the human images of charity in the intercourse of men and women, and particularly in marriage, are fundamentally like Freud's. Freud himself characteristically mocks the Christian injunction to love thy neighbor as thyself, but he nevertheless returns again and again in his writings to that state – akin to madness, he insists, but nevertheless universal – in which one person does love another as himself, the state of being in love; and the capacity truly to receive by giving in fact constitutes the goal informing his whole theory of libidinal development.

In *Civilization and Its Discontents* Freud remarks upon "the similarity between the process of civilization and the libidinal development of the individual."[2] I think that Shakespeare at least assumed, if he was not consciously interested in representing, a comparable analogy. In both his Greek and Roman plays, plays set in epochs, before the birth of Christ, which Elizabethans would have considered spiritually uncivilized,erotic energy has a regressive expression never found in the plays we have been discussing. In *Troilus and Cressida,* the war and the love-affair are repeatedly linked, and both are modulations of what one critic has called "oral narcissism"[3] – the "appetite" of which Ulysses speaks in his famous speech on order, the "universal wolf," that "doubly seconded with will and power, / Must make perforce an universal prey, / And last eat up himself" (I. 3. 121). It has often been speculated that Shakespeare wrote *Troilus and Cressida* with a performance by a children's company or Inn of Court in mind. The burlesque and ironic energies of the play are certainly more akin to the characteristic effects of the satirical comedies of the coterie theater than to the tragicomic conformations of *Measure for Measure* and *All's Well,* and it would have been typical of Shakespeare's genius to use the literal childishness of the actors to portray the profound folly and viciousness of a world in which grown-up men with grown-up power are in fact spiritual and psychic infants.

The Roman plays, in their preoccupation with identity, may be less infantile than adolescent – which, again, would be the psychic equivalent for Shakespeare of the age of civilization immediately preceding the birth of Christ. The erotic energy of a play like *Antony and Cleopatra* is hardly to be explained or enclosed, of course, by any psychic or theological label. It may not be entirely beside the point, however, to suggest that Antony and Cleopatra's love ultimately has the cadence more of fantasy than of dreams and that its wishes can never be represented as fulfilled because they belong to a past that is not immanent, but lost. Even Antony's great magnanimity, which constitutes the play's closest approximation to charity, is a memory that has little function in the present and no future. And the political world of the play, a world whose reality principle is the property of the notably unerotic Caesar, enforces the sense that the lovers' quest, though heroic, is also inescapably regressive and self-destructive.

There is an altogether different sense of the potentialities of erotic experience in the plays in which the relation between a man and a woman can be formed in the image of Christ's union with his congregation. There are, as we have seen, many different inflections of erotic love in *Othello, Much Ado About Nothing, Measure for Measure, All's Well That Ends Well,* and *Cymbeline,* depending upon the material Shakespeare is exploring and the generic logic of the particular play, but in all of them the ideal of a union in which a man loves his wife as himself brings with it an incandescent apprehension of the possibilities of generosity in the human psyche and spirit. We see this spiritual and psychic amplitude in the greatness of heart that animates Othello's jealousy as well as his love, and we see it, of course, in the imperishable charity that animates Desdemona's love for him. It is embodied in Dogberry's foolish dilation of language and spirit and it informs the literally wonderful scene in church in which Benedick and Beatrice, against all the evidence of their highly sophisticated senses, open themselves to one another, and declare that 'I' and "you" are one. There is more awareness of the limitations of erotic love in the problem comedies, but even in these plays, the selfishness of sexual appetite is represented as essentially a stage in the growth of young men, and that growth offers the promise, which is actualized in the chastity of the heroines, of a love illuminated by affection as well as sensuality and informed by creative as well as procreative energy. And in *Cymbeline,* in such a scene as that in which Posthumus forgives Imogen, romantic love incorporates the family and the entire human community in its erotic scope; and the structure of the play as a whole directly suggests "that civilization is a process in the service of Eros, whose purpose is to combine single human individuals, and after that families, then races, peoples and nations, into one great unity, the unity of mankind."[4]

All of these plays present experiences of erotic love that are continuous with those of charity, the love that stems from and is directed towards God. In a famous passage in his First Epistle to the Corinthians, St. Paul says of this love, "Thogh I speake with the tongues of men and Angels, and have not love, I am *as* sounding brasse, or a tinkling cymbal." He goes on to say that "It suffreth all things: it beleveth all things: it endureth all things," and he concludes:

> When I was a childe, I spake as a childe, I understode as a childe, I thoght as a childe: but when I became a man, I put away childish things.
> For now we se through a glasse darkely: but then *shal we se* face to face. Now I knowe in parte: but then shal I knowe even as I am knowen.
> And now abideth faith, hope & love, *even* these thre: but the chiefest of these is love.

(1 Cor. xiii,1,7,11–13)

Romantic love in Shakespearean drama is the human image of the charity that St. Paul describes: it has the same plenitude, the same belief and endurance, the same luminousness, the same vision. And it is most suggestive that, like St. Paul, Shakespeare should associate such love with the process of becoming a man, for not the least of the reasons Shakespeare's representations of romantic love are so abiding is that they express the most civilized as well as primitive of our erotic yearnings and show us how much the realization of our humanity consists of the development of our capacity to love.

# Notes

## Chapter 1   Introduction

1 Arthur Sherbo, ed., *Johnson on Shakespeare: The Yale Edition of the Works of Samuel Johnson*, 11 vols. to date (New Haven: Yale University Press, 1958-78), 7, p. 62.
2 Ibid., pp. 69-70.
3 Vladimir Nabokov, *Speak Memory* (New York: Putnam, 1970), p. 20.
4 There is some helpful scholarship on the impact of the morality plays on Shakespeare and Renaissance drama. See especially Bernard Spivack, *Shakespeare and the Allegory of Evil* (New York: Columbia University Press, 1958); T. W. Craik, *The Tudor Interlude* (Leicester: Humanities Press, 1958); and David Bevington, *From "Mankind" to Marlowe* (Cambridge, Mass.: Harvard University Press, 1962). Less has been written about the possible influence of the mystery drama. A recent chapter by Emrys Jones in *Origins of Shakespeare* (Oxford University Press, 1977) is important; and William Empson's brilliant analogies in *Some Versions of Pastoral* (London: Chatto and Windus, 1935) between the double plots of *The Second Shepherds' Play* and Renaissance plays are still extraordinarily fertile. See also F. D. Hoeniger's introduction to his New Arden edition of *Pericles* (London: Methuen, 1963) for material on the related issue of the influence of saint's play.
5 *Mount Tabor* (London, 1639), quoted in F. P. Wilson and G. K. Hunter, *The English Drama, 1485-1585* (London: Oxford University Press, 1969), pp. 76-77; and *"Mankind" to Marlowe*, pp. 13-14.
6 *The English Drama*, p. 77.
7 *Origins of Shakespeare*, addresses this issue directly, as does Glynne Wickham, *Early English Stages, 1300-1660*, 2 vols. (London: Routledge and Kegan Paul, 1959-71), 1, pp. 112-76.

181

## Othello

1 See Rosalie Colie, *Shakespeare's Living Art* (Princeton University Press, 1974), pp. 135–67.
2 John Booty, ed., *The Book of Common Prayer 1559* (Charlottesville: Folger Books, 1976), p. 297. The biblical text (Eph. v. 28–32) varies slightly in the Geneva translation. See also Gen. ii, 24.
3 Joan Rivière trans., "The Most Prevalent Form of Degradation in Erotic Life," in Philip Rieff, ed., *Freud: Sexuality and the Psychology of Love* (New York: Collier Books, 1963), pp. 59–61. All other references to Freud are to James Strachey, trans. and ed., *The Standard Edition of the Complete Psychological Works of Sigmund Freud*, 24 vols. (London: Hogarth Press, 1953–74).
4 A. P. Rossiter, *Angel With Horns* (New York: Theater Arts, 1961), p. 206.
5 W. H. Auden, *The Dyer's Hand* (New York: Random House, 1968), pp. 268–9.
6 All quotations from Shakespeare are from Peter Alexander's edition, *Shakespeare* (London: Collins, 1951).
7 Cordelia says to Lear:

> Good my lord,
> You have begot me, bred me, lov'd me; I
> Return those duties back as are right fit,
> Obey you, love you, and most honour you.
> Why have my sisters husbands, if they say
> They love you all? Haply, when I shall wed,
> That lord whose hand must take my plight shall carry
> Half my love with him, half my care and duty.
> Sure I shall never marry like my sisters,
> To love my father all.
>
> (I. 1. 94)

8 J. E. Spingarn, ed., *Critical Essays of the Seventeenth Century*, 3 vols. (London: Oxford University Press, 1908), 2, p. 221.
9 "What is symbolized as a virgin" in romance, Northrop Frye suggests, "is actually a human conviction, however expressed, that there is something at the core of one's infinitely fragile being which is not only immortal but has discovered the secret of invulnerability that eludes the tragic hero." *The Secular Scripture* (Cambridge, Mass.: Harvard University Press, 1976), p. 86. Though Desdemona herself is not invulnerable, her love is. Elizabethan theological writers commonly equated virginity and marital chastity. Henry Bullinger, for example, quoted St. John Chrysostom: "The first degree

of chastity is unspotted virginity; the second is faithful wedlock." *The Decades of Henry Bullinger*, Parker Society edition. 4 vols. (Cambridge University Press, 1849–52), 1, p. 402.

10 See Ernest Brennecke, "'Nay, That's Not Next!': The Significance of Desdemona's 'Willow Song,'" *Shakespeare Quarterly*, 4 (1953), pp. 35–8.

11 See Lawrence J. Ross, "World and Chrysolite in *Othello*," *Modern Language Notes*, 76 (1961), pp. 683–92.

12 See John E. Seaman, "Othello's Pearl," *Shakespeare Quarterly*, 19 (1968), pp. 81–5.

13 "Othello and Colour Prejudice," *Proceedings of the British Academy*, 53 (1967), pp. 139–63. Hunter's discussion of Othello's blackness is masterful, and I am very much indebted to it.

14 Northrop Frye, *Fools of Time* (University of Toronto Press, 1967), p. 102.

15 Quoted in Hunter, "Othello and Colour Prejudice," p. 153.

16 Thomas McFarland, *Tragic Meanings in Shakespeare* (New York: Random House, 1966), pp. 60–91; Barbara Heliodora C. De Mendonça, "*Othello* A Tragedy Built on a Comic Structure," *Shakespeare Survey* 21 (Cambridge University Press, 1968), pp. 31–8.

17 For an excellent discussion of the Elizabethan decorum of Othello's public behavior, see John Holloway, *The Story of the Night* (London: Routledge and Kegan Paul, 1961), pp. 40–2.

18 *Fools of Time*, p. 102; G. Wilson Knight, "The Othello Music" in *The Wheel of Fire* (London: Oxford University Press, 1930), pp. 107–131.

19 Freud, "On Narcissism: An Introduction," *Works*, 14, pp. 88, 100; "Femininity," 22, pp. 133–4.

20 Riviere's trans., "Degradation in Erotic Life," pp. 60–1; "On Narcissism," *Works*, 14, pp. 88, 100.

21 See Frederick Goldin, *The Mirror of Narcissus* (Ithaca, New York: Cornell University Press, 1967).

22 Northrop Frye, *A Natural Perspective* (New York: Columbia University Press, 1965), p. 132; *The Secular Scripture*, pp. 149, 153.

23 *The Wheel of Fire*, pp. 122–3.

24 F. R. Leavis, "Diabolic Intellect and the Noble Hero," *Scrutiny*, 6 (1937), pp. 264, 270. For a highly damaging analysis of Leavis's argument, see Holloway, *The Story of the Night*, pp. 155–65.

25 *Shakespeare and the Allegory of Evil*.

26 Leah Scragg, "Iago – Vice or Devil?" *Shakespeare Survey 21* (1968), pp. 53–65.

27 See Frye, *Fools of Time*, p. 103.

28 *The Dyer's Hand*, p. 266.

29 *Works*, 21, p. 144.
30 Rivière's trans., pp. 62, 65, 68.
31 John Florio, trans., *The Essayes of Michael Lord of Montaigne*, 3 vols. (London: J. M. Dent, 1910), 3, pp. 105, 72, 77, 106, 115, 75.

## Much Ado About Nothing

1 Edwin Wilson, ed., *Shaw on Shakespeare*, (Harmondsworth: Penguin, 1961), pp. 135–6.
2 Ibid., pp. 136–7.
3 Booty, ed., *Book of Common Prayer*, pp. 290–1, 297, 298–9.
4 "Group Psychology and the Analysis of the Ego," *Works*, 18, p. 112.
5 One of the few critics to take notice of Borachio's digression is David Ormerod, "Faith and Fashion in *Much Ado About Nothing*," *Shakespeare Survey 25* (Cambridge University Press, 1972), pp. 93–105. Ormerod discusses the conception of fashion in the play in some detail, but he does not consider Borachio's allusions or their implications.
6 *Book of Common Prayer*, p. 270.
7 "Verily, the mystery of our redemption by our Lord Jesus Christ is manifestly contained in the first precept of the ten commandments. For it is evident that the Israelite's free departure out of Egypt was a type or figure of the delivery of the whole compass of the earth, and of all the kingdoms of the world, which should be wrought by Christ our Lord, who hath now already set all the world free from the bondage of sin and hell." Bullinger, *Decades*, 1, pp. 218–19.
8 *Book of Common Prayer*, p. 276.
9 The Historie of Bel and of the dragon, 3, 5, and 1–22 passim.
10 See, e.g., "Peril of Idolatry" in *Sermons or Homilies Appointed to be Read in the Time of Queen Elizabeth* (London: Prayer-Book and Homily Society, 1817), pp. 209, 226–9.
11 Bullinger, *Decades*, 1, pp. 233–4.
12 As the liturgy of Matrimony itself suggests, Elizabethans tended to think of adultery and marriage as dialectically opposite states. In his handbook, *The Christen State of Matrimony* (London, 1541) Henry Bullinger devotes much of his discussion to the various positive purposes and duties of conjugal life, but very nearly a third of the treatise constitutes a sermon against the evils of whoredom and adultery. The subtitle of the book is itself revealing: "The origenall of holy wedlok: when / where / how and of whom it was instituted and ordeyned: what it is: how it ought to proceade: what be the occasions frute and commodities thereof. Contrary wyse / how shamefull and horrible a thing whoredome and adoutry is."
13 J. William Hebel ed. (New York: Facsimile Text Society, 1930), p. 199.

14 "Excess of Apparel" in *Homilies*, pp. 284, 289, 291.
15 For a most suggestive discussion of imagery of painted women in Shakespeare, see Edward Armstrong, *Shakespeare's Imagination* (London: Lindsay Drummond, 1946), pp. 66–71.
16 "On Narcissism," *Works*, 14, pp. 75, 85.
17 *Works*, 14, p. 149.
18 *Works*, 21, p. 66.
19 "The Interpretation of Dreams," *Works*, 5, p. 613.
20 Barbara K. Lewalski, "Love, Appearance, and Reality: Much Ado About Something," *Studies in English Literature*, 8 (1968), pp. 235–51.
21 In expounding his "most rare vision," his "dream, past the wit of man to say what dream it was," Bottom proclaims: "The eye of man hath not heard, the ear of man hath not seen, man's hand is not able to taste, his tongue to conceive, nor his heart to report, what my dream was" (IV. 1. 202–4, 210–14). His words are a clear, if unconscious, parody of 1 Cor. ii, 9: "But as it is written, The things which eye hathe not sene, nether eare hathe heard, nether came into mans heart, are, which God hathe prepared for them that love him." The text of the Bishops' Bible (London, 1568) is even closer to Bottom's speech "But as it is written: The eye hath not seene, and the eare hath not heard, neither have entred into the heart of man, the thynges which God hath prepared for them that love him."
22 *Works*, 8, p. 120.
23 Ibid., p. 236.
24 *Further Contributions to the Theory and Techniques of Psycho-Analysis* (New York: Basic Books, 1952), p. 344.
25 *Works*, 8, p. 130.
26 Ibid., p. 170.
27 Benedick's first reference occurs in his soliloquy after Beatrice bids him to come in to dinner (II. 3. 220); Leonato compares Benedick's complaint of love's "toothache" to a humour (III. 2. 25). Leonato himself later uses the image of a toothache in justifying his suffering over Hero's loss – "there was never yet philosopher / That could endure the toothache patiently" (V. 1. 35–36). The whole complex of images has a rather remarkable parallel in Freud, who uses the example of a toothache in his discussion of the problems of narcissism (*Works*, 14, p. 82).
28 "Humour," *Works*, 21, p. 161.
29 Ibid., pp. 162, 164.
30 Ibid., pp. 164–5.
31 "Civilization and its Discontents," *Works*, 21, p. 85.
32 Ibid., p. 64.
33 Ibid., p 68.

## Measure for Measure

1 I find it more convenient in making cross-references between the two plays to consider *Measure for Measure* first. *All's Well That Ends Well* is generally considered to be the earlier play, but the evidence is scant. My argument, in any case, does not assume that either play is an immature version of the other.

2 The earliest recorded complaint appears to be that of an anonymous late seventeenth-century writer, who remarked, "The play is something to serious for a Comedy yᵉ Plott is well layd but wants something to make it pleasant." See G. Blakemore Evans, "A Seventeenth-Century Reader of Shakespeare," *Review of English Studies*, 21 (1945), p. 274.

3 For critical histories of the play, see Jonathan R. Price, "*Measure for Measure* and the Critics: Towards a New Approach," *Shakespeare Quarterly*, 20 (1969), pp. 179–204; and Michael Jamieson, "The Problem Plays, 1920–1970: A Retrospect," *Shakespeare Survey 25* (Cambridge University Press, 1972), pp. 4–7.

4 The most notable exceptions, of course, are G. Wilson Knight, "*Measure for Measure* and the Gospels," in *The Wheel of Fire* (London: Oxford University Press, 1930); and R. W. Chambers, "The Jacobean Shakespeare and *Measure for Measure*, a British Academy lecture reprinted in *Man's Unconquerable Mind* (London: J. Cape, 1939). A more recent work focusing upon the religious background of the play is Darryl Gless, "*Measure for Measure*," the Law, and the Convent (Princeton University Press, 1979).

5 *Johnson on Shakespeare*, 7, p. 213.

6 Ibid., pp. 185, 184, and 177–8, respectively.

7 Ibid., p. 184.

8 I think A. P. Rossiter was a victim of these prejudices. They are particularly evident, for example, in *English Drama from Early Times to the Elizabethans* (London: Hutchinson's University Library, 1950), but it seems to me that they also subsume considerable portions of his argument about Shakespeare in *Angel With Horns*, including his treatment of *Measure for Measure* and *All's Well That Ends Well*.

9 *A New Postil . . . upon all the Sonday Gospelles*, 2 (London, 1566), sig. [Ddviii].

10 *A Postill . . . upon every gospell through the yeare* (London, 1550), sig. piiiiv.

11 Ibid., sigs. xiiii–xiiiiv.

12 *A Godly and Learned Exposition of Christs Sermon in the Mount* (Cambridge, 1608), sig. [Dd5].

13 Ibid., sigs. [Dd5]–Dd5v.

14 Portia continues with a direct reference to the Lord's Prayer: "we do pray for mercy, / And that same prayer doth teach us all to render / The deeds of mercy" (IV. 1. 195–7).

15 (Edinburgh, 1603), sig. [D8]. For a full discussion of the analogies between James I and the Duke, see David L. Stevenson, *The Achievement of Shakespeare's "Measure for Measure"* (Ithaca: Cornell University Press, 1966), pp. 134–66.

16 See Elizabeth M. Pope, "The Renaissance Background of *Measure for Measure*" *Shakespeare Survey 2* (Cambridge University Press, 1949), pp. 66–9.

17 Matt. vii, 9: "For what man is there among you, which if his sonne aske him bread, wolde give him a stone?" Lucio subsequently amplifies this theme in a lower key, when he remarks that Angelo is "a man whose blood / Is very snow-broth" (I. 4. 57–8) and that "Some report a sea-maid spawn'd him; some, that he was begot between two stock-fishes. But it is certain that when he makes water his urine is congeal'd ice; that I know to be true. And he is a motion generative; that's infallible" (III. 2. 100).

18 "Psycho-Analysis," *Works*, 18, p. 252

19 *Essayes*, 1, p. 88.

20 *Works*, 18, pp. 36, 38.

21 Ibid., p. 39.

22 Ibid., pp. 46, 57, 63.

23 *Essayes*, 1, p. 90.

24 Ibid., pp. 91, 93

25 For an illuminating discussion of the medieval history of the parable, see V. A. Kolve, "*Everyman* and the Parable of the Talents," in Jerome Taylor and Alan Nelson, eds., *Medieval English Drama* (University of Chicago Press, 1972), pp. 316–40.

26 The imagery of this passage is also related, quite subtly, to Mark v, 25–34. See Walter Whiter, *A Specimen of a Commentary on Shakespeare*, eds. Alan Over and Mary Bell (London: Methuen, 1967), pp. 203–04.

27 Hariett Hawkins, *Likenesses of Truth in Elizabethan and Restoration Drama* (Oxford University Press, 1972), p. 76. Essentially the same objections are raised by Rossiter in *Angel With Horns*, and even by Mary Lascelles at the end of her book, *Shakespeare's "Measure for Measure"* (London: Athlone Press, 1953).

28 Augustine Marlorate, *A Catholike and Ecclesiastical exposition of the holy Gospell after S. John* (London, 1575), sig. [Bb3]. Marlorate's discussion of temptation occurs in his exposition of the parable of the woman taken in adultery, a parable that is itself relevant to *Measure for Measure*.

29 *Exposition of Christs Sermon in the Mount*, sigs. Cc6v–[Cc7].

30 The alleged split in *Measure for Measure*, a shibboleth of modern criticism, is also a prime instance of the failure to understand the play as a theatrical text, for even a director who is dissatisfied with the play has no difficulty with the Duke's intervention in Act III. Despite a pronounced lack of sympathy with the play's conclusion, for example, John Barton has testified that: "One thing, however, did seem to emerge in rehearsal and performance. It has often been pointed out how, on reading the play, one finds it splitting down the middle. At the point Isabella leaves Claudio after her interview with him in prison, and is left alone with the Duke, the level of writing changes. The Duke for the first time goes into prose, and into plotting the bedtrick; and the play, which has in the first half been poetically intense and psychologically subtle, is then worked out on a lower, almost fairy-tale, level. The change is obvious enough in the study; but in the theatre, I think the difference disappears. This is because the actors, if they have brought their characters to life in exploring the first half, can carry through that life into the play's more superficial resolution. I felt, in fact, that what seemed a problem in the study largely melted away in the theatre, when those characters were embodied by living actors." ["Directing Problem Plays: John Barton talks to Gareth Lloyd Evans," *Shakespeare Survey 25* (Cambridge University Press, 1972), p. 65.]
31 *Appreciations* (London, 1889), p. 177.
32 *Compendium* to *Il Pastor Fido*, Allan H. Gilbert, trans., *Literary Criticism: Plato to Dryden* (New York: American Book Company, 1940), p. 511.
33 For a more extensive discussion of these developments, see Arthur Kirsch, *Jacobean Dramatic Perspectives* (Charlottesville: University Press of Virginia, 1972), pp. 7–15, 52–74.
34 The theatrical self-consciousness of this play has been much discussed, but see especially Francis Fergusson, *The Human Image in Dramatic Literature* (New York: Doubleday, 1957), pp. 138–43.
35 It is also an idea to which much recent criticism seems especially hostile. Philip Edwards, *Shakespeare and the Confines of Art* (London: Methuen, 1968), p. 118, says of the Duke's reasoning: "God works in mysterious ways, but this beats all – willingly to cause despair in order to show the beauty of divine consolation." It is odd, though symptomatic, that Edwards should at the same time declare that "Modern criticism has established beyond disproof" that there is in *Measure for Measure* "a Christian or near-Christian pattern of providence and redemption," "a religious rhythm," a plot whose movement "can certainly be an emblem of achieving grace" (p. 109). For

further discussions of Shakespeare's use of the idea of *felix culpa*, see the chapters on *All's Well That Ends Well* and *Cymbeline*.

36 For an excellent treatment of this point, see Michael Goldman, *Shakespeare and the Energies of Drama* (Princeton University Press, 1972), pp. 164–74.

37 *Appreciations*, p. 189.

## All's Well That Ends Well

1 For a critical and stage history of *All's Well*, see Joseph G. Price, *The Unfortunate Comedy* (Liverpool University Press, 1968).

2 The word is G. K. Hunter's, in his introduction to the New Arden edition of the play (London: Methuen, 1959), p. xxix; most of the evidences of strain that I mention are discussed at length by Hunter.

3 Cf., e.g., W. W. Lawrence, *Shakespeare's Problem Comedies* (New York: Macmillan, 1931), pp. 43–79, who argues that Helena should be understood as a romantic heroine facing essentially conventional (and medieval) tasks, and Clifford Leech, "The Theme of Ambition in *All's Well*," *English Literary History*, 21 (1954), pp. 17–29, who believes that Helena is tainted by ambition.

4 Preface to *The Faithful Shepherdess* (London, ca. 1609).

5 See *Jacobean Dramatic Perspectives*, pp. 10–12.

6 *Johnson on Shakespeare*, 7, p. 404.

7 *Angel with Horns*, p. 92.

8 *Johnson on Shakespeare*, 7, p. 400.

9 *Angel with Horns*, p. 91.

10 Ibid., pp. 98–9.

11 *Essayes*, 3, p. 73.

12 Ibid., p. 72.

13 *Angel With Horns*, p. 99.

14 *Essayes* 3, pp. 62–3.

15 Ibid., pp. 65–66, 68, 70.

16 "Of Repenting," *Essayes*, 3, p. 23.

17 *Essayes* 3, pp. 76, 81, 86, 88.

17 Ibid., p. 106.

19 Ibid., pp. 126, 127.

20 Ibid., p. 125.

21 Ibid., p. 115.

22 Ibid., pp. 118, 123.

23 John Farmer, ed., *The World and the Child*, (London: Tudor Facsimile Text, 1909), sig. Aiiiv; David Bevington, ed., *Mankind* in *The Macro Plays*, New York: Johnson Reprint Corporation, 1972), l. 295; Be-

vington, ed., *The Castle of Perseverance* in *The Macro Plays*, ll. 1058–61; Robert Ramsay, ed., *Magnyfycence*, Early English Text Society (London: Kegan Paul, Trench, Trübner, 1908), ll. 845–6, and 829–61 passim; Bevington, ed., *Wisdom* in *The Macro Plays*, ll. 380, and 551–620 passim. See also Pride's advice to Youthe in Bang and McKerrow, eds., *The Enterlude of Youth*, (London: David Nutt, 1905), ll. 344–8.

24 Richard David, "Plays Pleasant and Unpleasant," *Shakespeare Survey 8* (Cambridge University Press, 1955), p. 135.

25 *A Natural Perspective*, pp. 105–6.

26 *The Book of Common Prayer 1559*, pp. 290, 297.

27 See, e.g., Edwards, *Shakespeare and the Confines of Art*, pp. 113–15.

28 For a discussion of the relation of *All's Well* to contemporary prodigal plays and themes, see Robert Y. Turner, "Dramatic Convention in *All's Well That Ends Well*," *PMLA*, 75 (1960), pp. 497–502; and Robert G. Hunter, *Shakespeare and the Comedy of Forgiveness* (New York: Columbia University Press, 1965), pp. 106–31.

29 As I have also suggested, Johnson's response (as well as Rossiter's) is governed as much by his discomfort with tragicomedy as by the nature of his own beliefs. I think that despite his apparent preference for Shakespeare's comedies, it was really the tragedies that moved Johnson most deeply and that elicited the kind of appreciation of Shakespeare that is evident in the passages from the "Preface," which I quoted in Chapter 1.

## Cymbeline

1 See Homer Swander, "*Cymbeline* and the 'Blameless Hero,'" *English Literary History*, 31 (1964), pp. 259–70.

2 Marjorie Garber, *Dream in Shakespeare: From Metaphor to Metamorphosis* (New Haven: Yale University Press, 1974), pp. 157–63, calls attention to these speeches, but she does not focus in detail upon the mechanisms of dream-work themselves. The logic and mechanisms of dream-work are discussed, suggestively, but also indiscriminately, by Murray Schwartz, "Between Fantasy and Imagination, A Psychological Exploration of *Cymbeline*," in *Psychoanalysis and Literary Process*, ed. Frederick Crews (Cambridge, Mass.: Winthrop Publishers, 1970), pp. 219–83.

3 The doubling of Posthumus and Cloten is discussed, exclusively in moral terms, by James Siemon, "Noble Virtue in *Cymbeline*, *Shakespeare Survey 29* (Cambridge University Press, 1976), pp. 51–61. Some of the psychic implications of this doubling are considered by Schwartz, "Between Fantasy and Imagination," pp. 262–4, and more

briefly by R. G. Hunter, *Shakespeare and the Comedy of Forgiveness*, p. 158; Howard Felperin, *Shakespearean Romance* (Princeton University Press, 1972), p. 186; and Leslie Fiedler, *The Stranger in Shakespeare* (New York: Stein and Day, 1972), pp. 243-44.

4 See note by J. M. Nosworthy, New Arden ed. of *Cymbeline* (London: Methuen, 1955), pp. 220-2.

5 See Homer Swander, "*Cymbeline*: Religious Idea and Dramatic Design," in McNeir and Greenfield, eds., *Pacific Coast Studies in Shakespeare*, (Eugene, Oregon: University of Oregon Books, 1966), pp. 255-6.

6 For discussions of the political and historical resonances of *Cymbeline*, see Emrys Jones, "Stuart *Cymbeline*," *Essays in Criticism*, 11 (1961), pp. 84-99; and J. P. Brockbank, "History and Histrionics in *Cymbeline*," *Shakespeare Survey 11* (Cambridge University Press, 1958), pp. 42-9.

7 *A Natural Perspective*, pp. 66-7. Frye's point was anticipated by Robin Moffet, "*Cymbeline* and the Nativity," *Shakespeare Quarterly*, 13 (1962), pp. 207-18.

8 The religious configurations of *Cymbeline* are discussed by Hunter, *Comedy of Forgiveness*, pp. 142-84; and by Swander, "*Cymbeline*: Religious Idea and Dramatic Design," pp. 243-62.

9 "The Interpretation of Dreams," *Works*, 5, p. 608.

10 "Revision of the Theory of Dreams," *Works*, 22, pp. 18-19.

11 Because there is presently a disposition among psychoanalytic writers to question the usefulness of the concept of the dream-wish in the interpretation of dreams, it is particularly important to recognize Freud's own stress upon the distinction between the dream-wish and the actual dream-work. He added a cautionary note on the point to the 1925 edition of "The Interpretation of Dreams": "I used at one time to find it extraordinarily difficult to accustom readers to the distinction between the manifest content of dreams and the latent dream-thoughts. Again and again arguments and objections would be brought up based upon some uninterpreted dream in the form in which it had been retained in the memory, and the need to interpret it would be ignored. But now that analysts at least have become reconciled to replacing the manifest dream by the meaning revealed by its interpretation, many of them have become guilty of falling into another confusion, which they cling to with equal obstinacy. They seek to find the essence of dreams in their latent content and in so doing they overlook the distinction between the latent dream-thoughts and the dream-work. At bottom, dreams are nothing other than a particular *form* of thinking, made possible by the

conditions of the state of sleep. It is the *dream-work* which creates that form, and it alone is the essence of dreaming – the explanation of its peculiar nature" (*Works*, 5, pp. 506–7).

12 See, e.g., Lytton Strachey, "Shakespeare's Final Period," in *Books and Characters* (London: Chatto and Windus, 1922); and F. R. Leavis, "The Criticism of Shakespeare's Late Plays," in *The Common Pursuit* (London: Chatto and Windus, 1952).

13 *Works*, 5, p. 621.

14 *Faerie Queene*, 7, vii, 58, de Selincourt, ed., *Poetical Works* (London: Oxford University Press, 1912), p. 406.

15 Frank Kermode, *Shakespeare: The Final Plays* (London: Longmans, Green, 1963), p. 22.

16 *Johnson on Shakespeare*, 8, p. 908.

17 *Prefaces to Shakespeare*, 2 vols. (Princeton University Press, 1946), 1, p. 539.

18 *Works*, 5, p. 460.

19 *Prefaces*, 1, pp. 466–7.

20 Ibid., p. 498.

21 Arthur Kirsch, "*Cymbeline* and Coterie Dramaturgy," *English Literary History*, 34 (1967), pp. 285–306.

## Chapter 7   Conclusion

1 For an illuminating study of analogies between Freudian and Christian thought on this issue as well as others, see Sharon MacIsaac, *Freud and Original Sin* (New York: Paulist Press, 1974).

2 *Works*, 21, p. 97.

3 See Philip Slater's brilliant psychoanalytic study of Greek culture, *The Glory of Hera* (Boston: Beacon Press, 1968). Slater himself does not discuss Shakespeare, but his analysis has suggestive applications to both the Greek and Roman plays.

4 "Civilization and Its Discontents," *Works*, 21, p. 122.

# Index

apparel, 47–53, 128–31, 154–6, 159–61;
   and Vice characters, 52, 129–31
Auden, W. H., 11–12, 35–6
Augustine, St., 34

Bandello, Matteo, 174, 175
Baptism, liturgy of, 48, 161
Barton, John, 188n30
Becon, Thomas 76
Bible
   Bel and the Dragon (Apocrypha), 3,
      5: 49
   1 Cor. i, 17–20, 27: 60
   1 Cor. ii, 9: 185n21
   1 Cor. vi, 31: 52–3
   1 Cor. x, 1–13: 48
   1 Cor. xiii, 1, 7, 11–13: 180
   Eph. iv, 22, 24: 160–1
   Eph. v, 28–32: 10, 32, 140
   Ex. xiv, 27: 48
   Gen. ii, 24: 182n2
   Heb. xi, 1: 59
   Luke vi, 36–42: 75–7, 79
   Luke xix, 12–27: 94–7
   Matt. vii, 1–5 75, 77–8, 79, 158
   Matt. vii, 9: 187n17
   Matt. xiii, 45–6: 18
   Matt. xvi, 25: 92
   Matt. xviii, 23–35: 76, 77
   Matt. xxv, 14–30: 94–7
   1 Pet. iii, 1–3: 44, 52, 54
   Ps. 67, 138: 44
   Rev. xxi, 20: 18
   Rom. vii, 14–15, 20, 23: 81, 176–7
   Song of Songs: 20, 26
Blackfriars theater, 171
Boas, Frederick 71
Boccaccio, Giovanni, 121, 127, 174, 175,
   176

Bullinger, Henry, 49–50, 182–3n9,
   184n7, 184n12

Castle of Perseverance. 5–6, 130
Charles I, King, 131
Cinthio, Geraldi, 174–5, 176
Corvinus, Antonius. 77
Cradle of Security, 3–4

Donne, John, Biathanatos, 50
dreams, processes of, 7–8, 153, 163–
   70, 191–2n11

Edwards, Philip, 188n35

Ferenczi, Sandor, 62
Fletcher John, 113–14, 171
fortunate fall, paradox of, 106, 114–15,
   162–3, 165, 171
Freud, Sigmund
   Beyond the Pleasure Principle: 92–3
   Civilization and Its Discontents: 37, 59,
      69, 177, 178
   "Degradation in Erotic Life": 11, 26,
      37–8, 177
   "Femininity": 25
   "Group Psychology and the
      Analysis of the Ego": 44–5
   "Humour": 67–8, 69
   Interpretation of Dreams: 59, 163–70,
      191–2n11
   Jokes and Their Relation to the Uncon-
      scious: 61, 64
   "On Narcissism": 24–5, 26, 57
   "Psycho-Analysis": 84
   "Revision of the Theory of
      Dreams": 164
Frye, Northrop, 23, 26, 138, 152, 161

Granville-Barker, Harley, 169, 170–1
Guarini, Giovanni, Battista, 104–5, 113–14, 115

Hall, Bishop Joseph, 20
Homilies, Book of, 49, 52–3
Hordern, Michael, 132
Hunter, G. K., 19, 21

idolatry, 11, 21, 35, 49–50

James I, King, Basilicon Doron, 79
Johnson, Samuel, 1, 73, 74, 116, 117, 118, 143, 168

Knight, G. Wilson, 23, 26

Leavis, F. R., 27
Lyly, John, Campaspe, 157

Magnificence, 130
Mankind, 130
Marston, John, 114, 171
Matrimony, liturgy of, 10, 42, 43–4, 52, 140–1, 145, 160
Miller, Jonathan, 71
Montaigne, Michel de
  "Of Repenting": 124
  "That to Philosophie, is to learne how to die": 91, 93–4
  "Upon Some Verses of Virgil": 38–9, 122–7, 133, 136, 137, 141, 142, 143
morality drama, 3–6, 52, 129–31
Mozart, Wolfgang Amadeus, Don Giovanni, 41
mystery drama, 6–8, 101–2, 163, 166–7

Nabakov, Vladimir, Speak Memory, 2
narcissism, primary, 11, 24–5, 59, 65, 69, 177–8

Pater, Walter, 104, 107
Perkins, William, 77–8, 101

Roman de la Rose, 49
Rossiter, A. P., 11, 117, 118, 122, 123, 137, 143
Rymer, Thomas, 14, 34

Second Shepherds' Play, 7, 8, 101–2, 166
Shakespeare, William
  All's Well That Ends Well: 9, 52, 93, 94, 101–2, 105, 108–43, 144, 145, 146, 149, 150, 152, 155, 158, 162, 174, 175, 178, 179
  Antony and Cleopatra: 178–9
  As You Like It: 68
  Cymbeline: 8, 9, 52, 55, 142, 144–73, 174, 176, 179–80
  King Lear: 14
  Measure for Measure: 9, 71–107, 110, 115, 136, 144, 145, 146, 149, 150, 152, 158, 174, 175–6, 178, 179
  Midsummer Night's Dream: 61, 68, 85
  Much Ado About Nothing: 8, 9, 40–70, 129, 144, 145, 148, 150–1, 155, 156, 158, 162, 174, 175, 176, 179
  Othello: 6, 9, 10–39, 122, 125, 144, 145, 146, 147, 148, 150, 152, 156, 159, 174–5, 179
  Pericles: 167
  Taming of the Shrew: 111
  Tempest: 13, 106, 115, 166
  Troilus and Cressida: 11, 90, 178
  Winter's Tale: 165, 167, 172
Shaw, George Bernard, 40–1, 110
Spenser, Edmund, 166–7
Spivack, Bernard, 28

talents, parable of, 85–6, 94–7, 136, 149–50, 161

Whetstone, George, Promos and Cassandra, 80
Willis, Ralph, 3–4
Wilson, F. P., 4
Wisdom, 130
World and the Child, 130